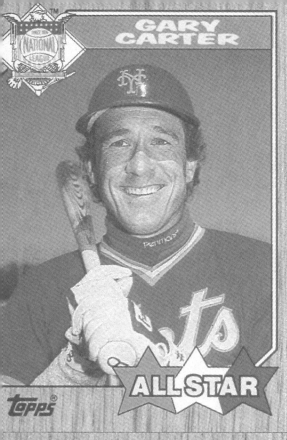

GARY CARTER

ALL STAR

Topps

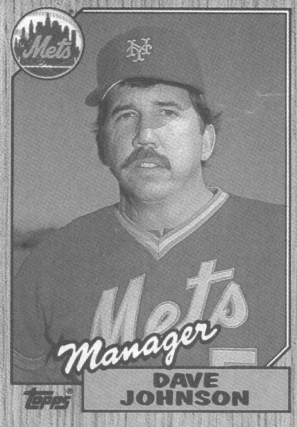

DAVE JOHNSON

Topps

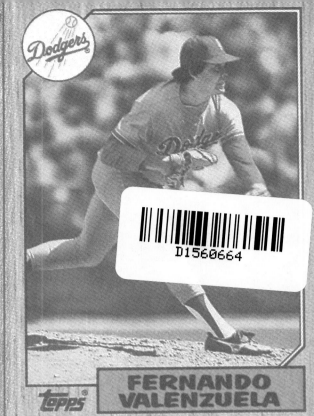

FERNANDO VALENZUELA

Topps

JOE CARTER

Topps

TONY GWYNN

ALL STAR

Topps

RICKEY HENDERSON

Topps

DON MATTINGLY

Topps

JOSE CANSECO

Topps

TOPPS ALL-STAR ROOKIE

CAL RIPKEN

ALL STAR

THE COMPLETE PICTURE COLLECTION

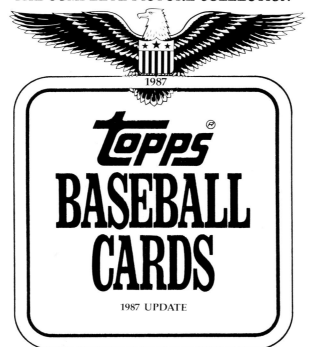

1987

topps®
BASEBALL
CARDS

1987 UPDATE

THE COMPLETE PICTURE COLLECTION

BASEBALL CARDS

UPDATE 1987

Text by
Red Foley

WARNER BOOKS

Warner Communications Company

Warner Books Inc., 666 Fifth Avenue, New York, NY 10103
A Warner Communications Company

Designed and produced by MBKA, Inc.
Suite 8L, 340 East 80th Street, New York, NY 10021
Printed and bound in Hong Kong by
Mandarin Offset
First Printing: November 1987
10 9 8 7 6 5 4 3 2 1

CONTENTS

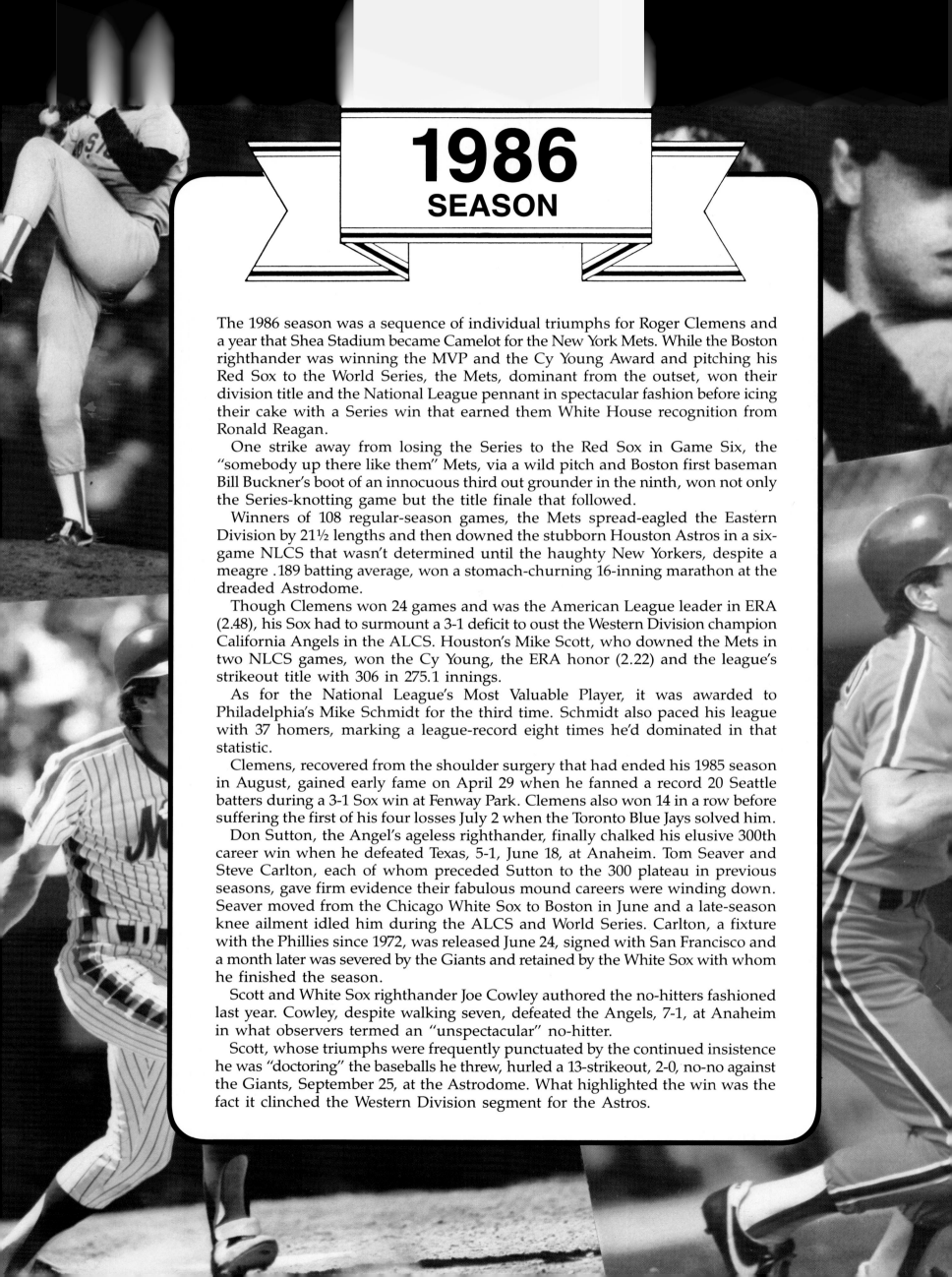

1986
SEASON

The 1986 season was a sequence of individual triumphs for Roger Clemens and a year that Shea Stadium became Camelot for the New York Mets. While the Boston righthander was winning the MVP and the Cy Young Award and pitching his Red Sox to the World Series, the Mets, dominant from the outset, won their division title and the National League pennant in spectacular fashion before icing their cake with a Series win that earned them White House recognition from Ronald Reagan.

One strike away from losing the Series to the Red Sox in Game Six, the "somebody up there like them" Mets, via a wild pitch and Boston first baseman Bill Buckner's boot of an innocuous third out grounder in the ninth, won not only the Series-knotting game but the title finale that followed.

Winners of 108 regular-season games, the Mets spread-eagled the Eastern Division by 21½ lengths and then downed the stubborn Houston Astros in a six-game NLCS that wasn't determined until the haughty New Yorkers, despite a meagre .189 batting average, won a stomach-churning 16-inning marathon at the dreaded Astrodome.

Though Clemens won 24 games and was the American League leader in ERA (2.48), his Sox had to surmount a 3-1 deficit to oust the Western Division champion California Angels in the ALCS. Houston's Mike Scott, who downed the Mets in two NLCS games, won the Cy Young, the ERA honor (2.22) and the league's strikeout title with 306 in 275.1 innings.

As for the National League's Most Valuable Player, it was awarded to Philadelphia's Mike Schmidt for the third time. Schmidt also paced his league with 37 homers, marking a league-record eight times he'd dominated in that statistic.

Clemens, recovered from the shoulder surgery that had ended his 1985 season in August, gained early fame on April 29 when he fanned a record 20 Seattle batters during a 3-1 Sox win at Fenway Park. Clemens also won 14 in a row before suffering the first of his four losses July 2 when the Toronto Blue Jays solved him.

Don Sutton, the Angel's ageless righthander, finally chalked his elusive 300th career win when he defeated Texas, 5-1, June 18, at Anaheim. Tom Seaver and Steve Carlton, each of whom preceded Sutton to the 300 plateau in previous seasons, gave firm evidence their fabulous mound careers were winding down. Seaver moved from the Chicago White Sox to Boston in June and a late-season knee ailment idled him during the ALCS and World Series. Carlton, a fixture with the Phillies since 1972, was released June 24, signed with San Francisco and a month later was severed by the Giants and retained by the White Sox with whom he finished the season.

Scott and White Sox righthander Joe Cowley authored the no-hitters fashioned last year. Cowley, despite walking seven, defeated the Angels, 7-1, at Anaheim in what observers termed an "unspectacular" no-hitter.

Scott, whose triumphs were frequently punctuated by the continued insistence he was "doctoring" the baseballs he threw, hurled a 13-strikeout, 2-0, no-no against the Giants, September 25, at the Astrodome. What highlighted the win was the fact it clinched the Western Division segment for the Astros.

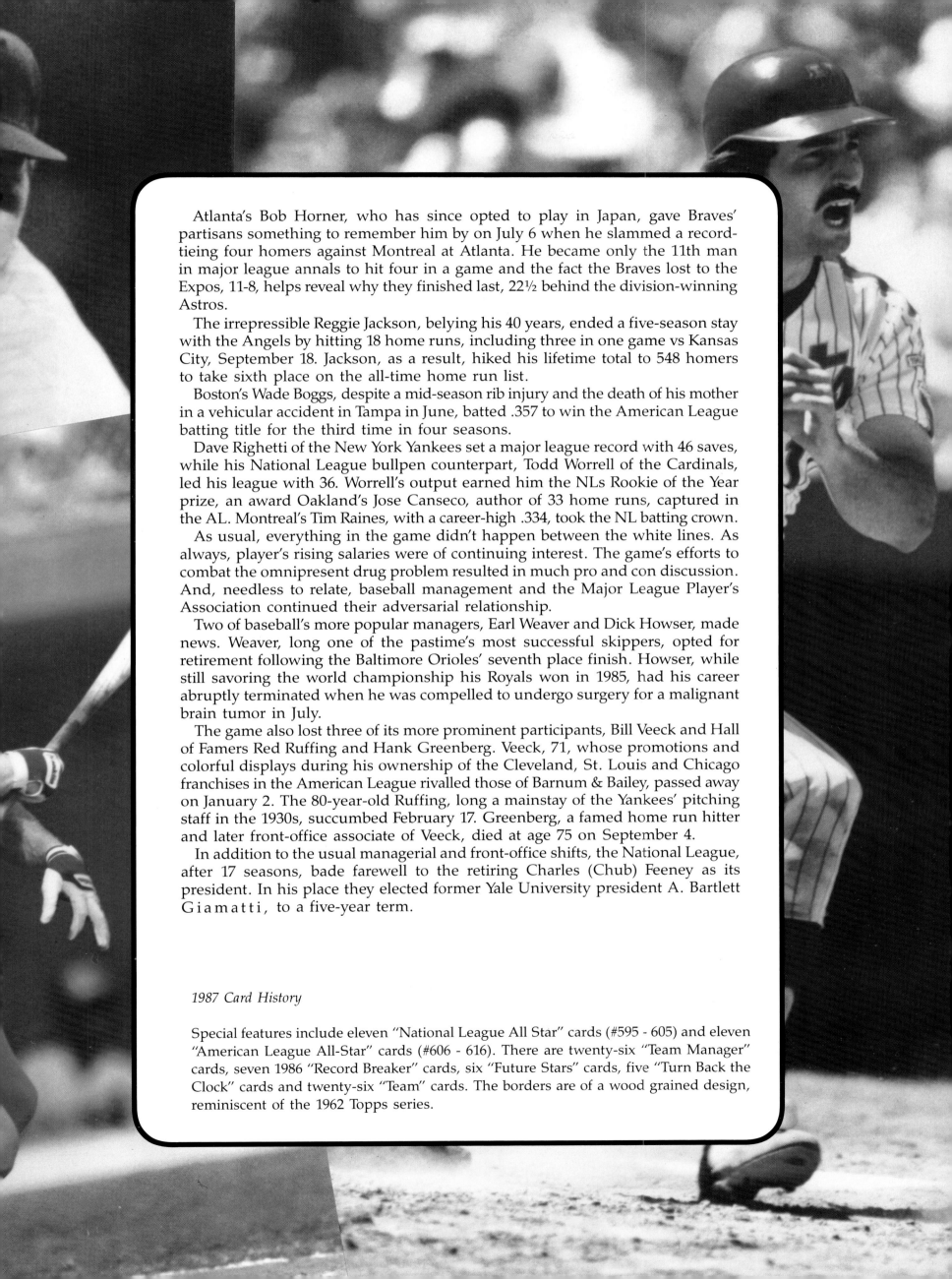

Atlanta's Bob Horner, who has since opted to play in Japan, gave Braves' partisans something to remember him by on July 6 when he slammed a record-tieing four homers against Montreal at Atlanta. He became only the 11th man in major league annals to hit four in a game and the fact the Braves lost to the Expos, 11-8, helps reveal why they finished last, 22½ behind the division-winning Astros.

The irrepressible Reggie Jackson, belying his 40 years, ended a five-season stay with the Angels by hitting 18 home runs, including three in one game vs Kansas City, September 18. Jackson, as a result, hiked his lifetime total to 548 homers to take sixth place on the all-time home run list.

Boston's Wade Boggs, despite a mid-season rib injury and the death of his mother in a vehicular accident in Tampa in June, batted .357 to win the American League batting title for the third time in four seasons.

Dave Righetti of the New York Yankees set a major league record with 46 saves, while his National League bullpen counterpart, Todd Worrell of the Cardinals, led his league with 36. Worrell's output earned him the NLs Rookie of the Year prize, an award Oakland's Jose Canseco, author of 33 home runs, captured in the AL. Montreal's Tim Raines, with a career-high .334, took the NL batting crown.

As usual, everything in the game didn't happen between the white lines. As always, player's rising salaries were of continuing interest. The game's efforts to combat the omnipresent drug problem resulted in much pro and con discussion. And, needless to relate, baseball management and the Major League Player's Association continued their adversarial relationship.

Two of baseball's more popular managers, Earl Weaver and Dick Howser, made news. Weaver, long one of the pastime's most successful skippers, opted for retirement following the Baltimore Orioles' seventh place finish. Howser, while still savoring the world championship his Royals won in 1985, had his career abruptly terminated when he was compelled to undergo surgery for a malignant brain tumor in July.

The game also lost three of its more prominent participants, Bill Veeck and Hall of Famers Red Ruffing and Hank Greenberg. Veeck, 71, whose promotions and colorful displays during his ownership of the Cleveland, St. Louis and Chicago franchises in the American League rivalled those of Barnum & Bailey, passed away on January 2. The 80-year-old Ruffing, long a mainstay of the Yankees' pitching staff in the 1930s, succumbed February 17. Greenberg, a famed home run hitter and later front-office associate of Veeck, died at age 75 on September 4.

In addition to the usual managerial and front-office shifts, the National League, after 17 seasons, bade farewell to the retiring Charles (Chub) Feeney as its president. In his place they elected former Yale University president A. Bartlett Giamatti, to a five-year term.

1987 Card History

Special features include eleven "National League All Star" cards (#595 - 605) and eleven "American League All-Star" cards (#606 - 616). There are twenty-six "Team Manager" cards, seven 1986 "Record Breaker" cards, six "Future Stars" cards, five "Turn Back the Clock" cards and twenty-six "Team" cards. The borders are of a wood grained design, reminiscent of the 1962 Topps series.

TRADED SERIES 1986

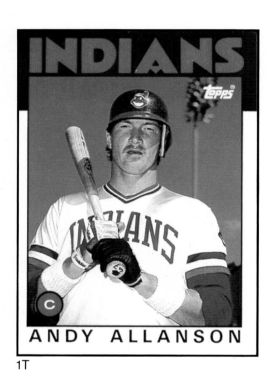

ANDY ALLANSON

1T

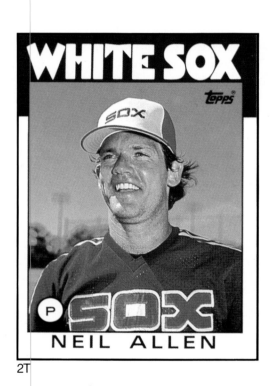

NEIL ALLEN

2T

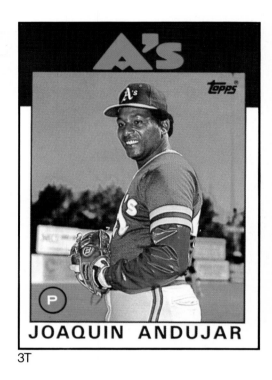

JOAQUIN ANDUJAR

3T

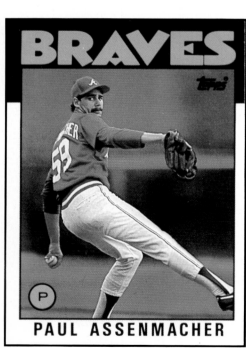

PAUL ASSENMACHER

4T

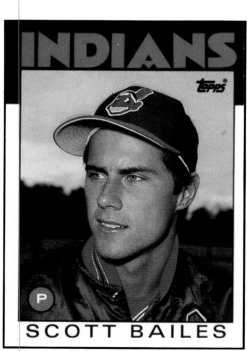

SCOTT BAILES

5T

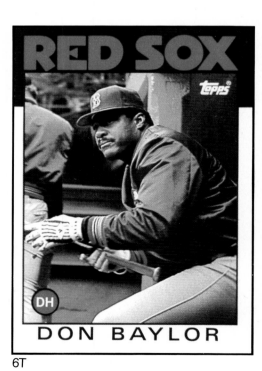

DON BAYLOR

6T

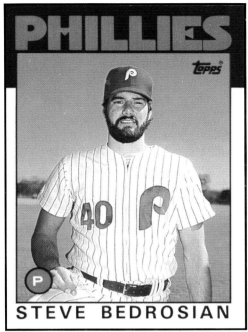

PHILLIES

STEVE BEDROSIAN

7T

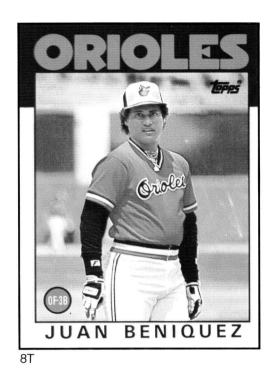

ORIOLES

JUAN BENIQUEZ

8T

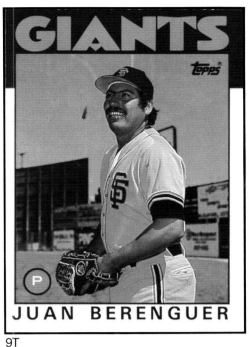

GIANTS

JUAN BERENGUER

9T

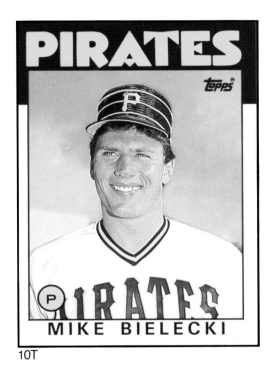

PIRATES

MIKE BIELECKI

10T

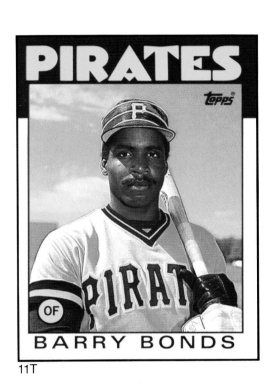

PIRATES

BARRY BONDS

11T

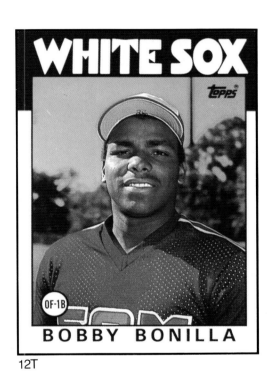

WHITE SOX

BOBBY BONILLA

12T

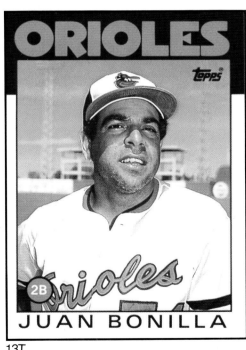

ORIOLES

JUAN BONILLA

13T

ORIOLES

RICH BORDI

14T

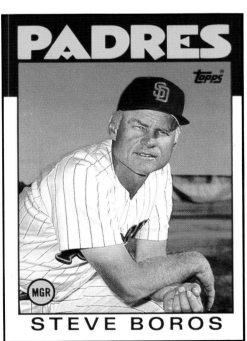

PADRES

STEVE BOROS

15T

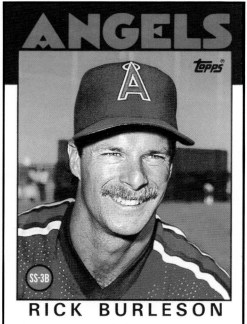

ANGELS

RICK BURLESON

SS-3B

16T

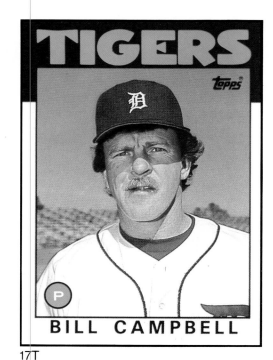

TIGERS

BILL CAMPBELL

P

17T

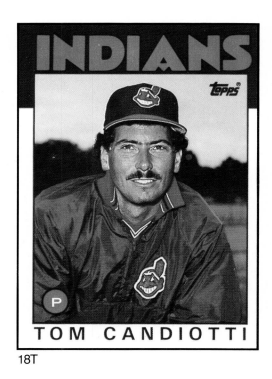

INDIANS

TOM CANDIOTTI

P

18T

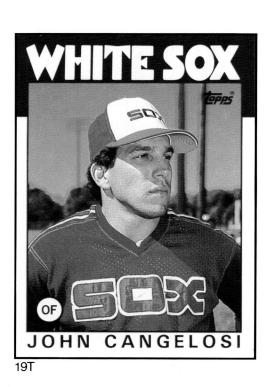

WHITE SOX

JOHN CANGELOSI

OF

19T

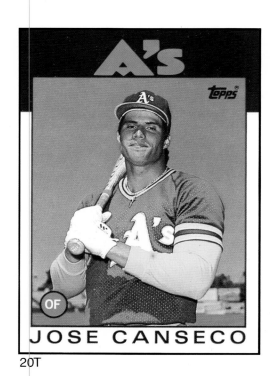

A's

JOSE CANSECO

OF

20T

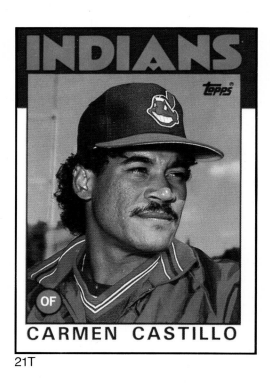

INDIANS

CARMEN CASTILLO

OF

21T

BREWERS

RICK CERONE

C

22T

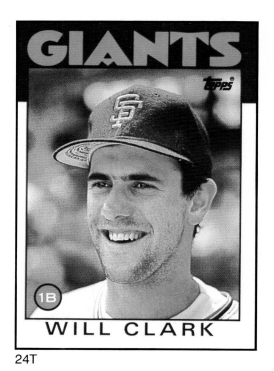

BLUE JAYS

JOHN CERUTTI

P

23T

GIANTS

WILL CLARK

1B

24T

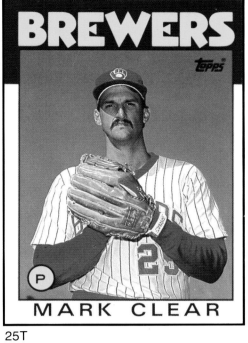

BREWERS

MARK CLEAR

P

25T

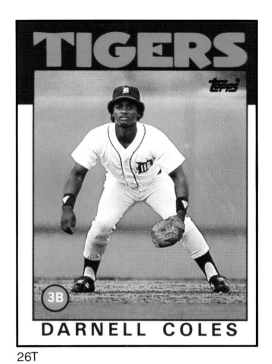

TIGERS

DARNELL COLES

3B

26T

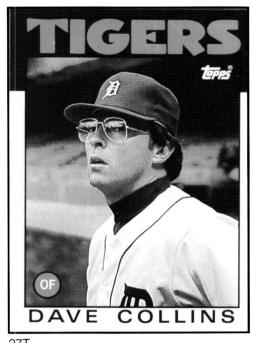

TIGERS

DAVE COLLINS

OF

27T

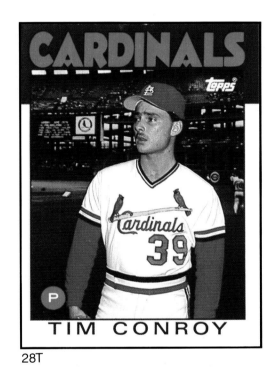

CARDINALS

TIM CONROY

P

28T

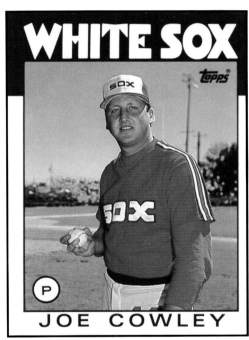

WHITE SOX

JOE COWLEY

P

29T

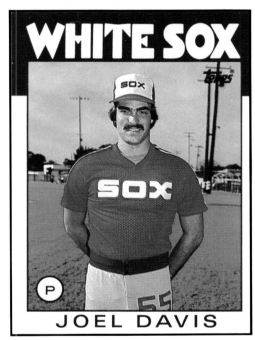

WHITE SOX

JOEL DAVIS

P

30T

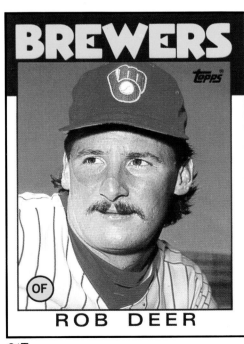

BREWERS

ROB DEER

OF

31T

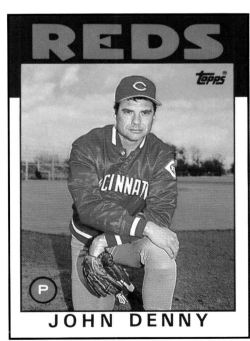

REDS

JOHN DENNY

P

32T

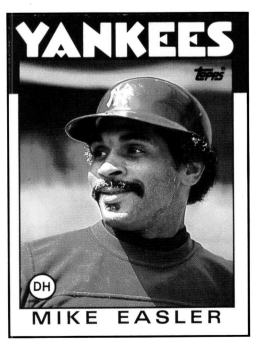

YANKEES

MIKE EASLER

DH

33T

BLUE JAYS

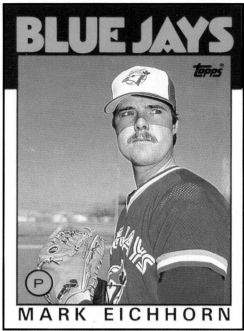

MARK EICHHORN

34T

ROYALS

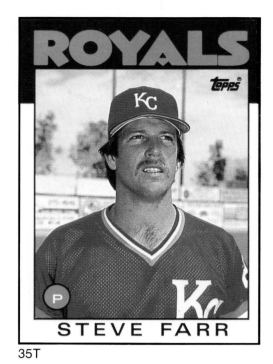

STEVE FARR

35T

RANGERS

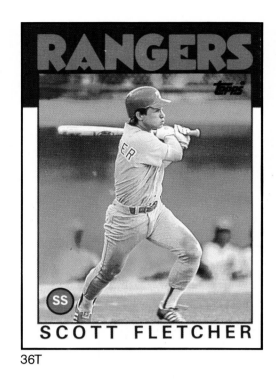

SCOTT FLETCHER

36T

ANGELS

TERRY FORSTER

37T

CUBS

TERRY FRANCONA

38T

WHITE SOX

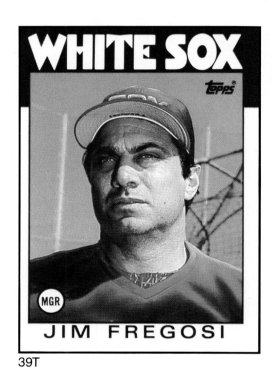

JIM FREGOSI

39T

EXPOS

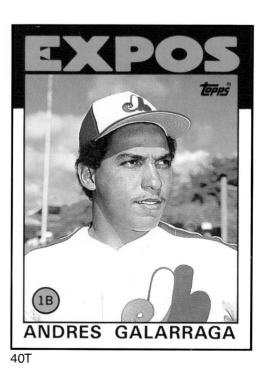

ANDRES GALARRAGA

40T

BRAVES

KEN GRIFFEY

41T

REDS

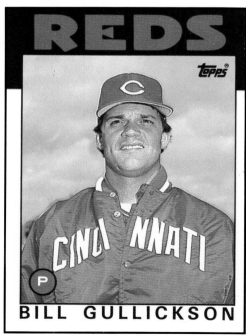

BILL GULLICKSON

42T

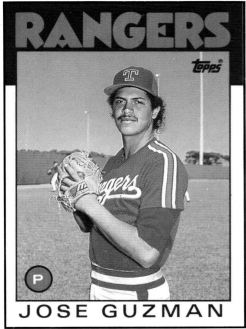

RANGERS

JOSE GUZMAN

43T

A's

MOOSE HAAS

44T

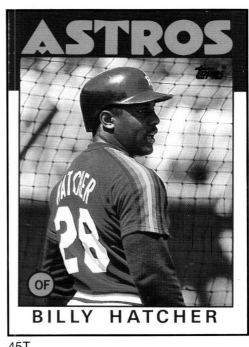

ASTROS

BILLY HATCHER

45T

CARDINALS

MIKE HEATH

46T

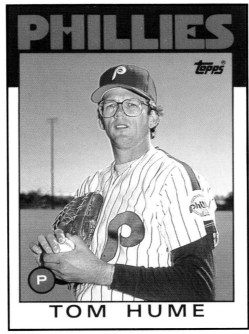

PHILLIES

TOM HUME

47T

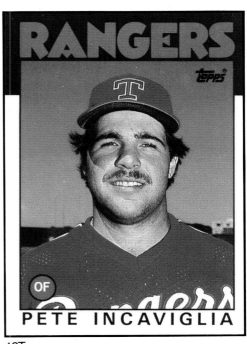

RANGERS

PETE INCAVIGLIA

48T

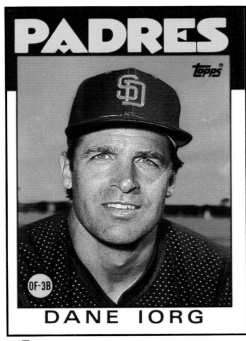

PADRES

DANE IORG

49T

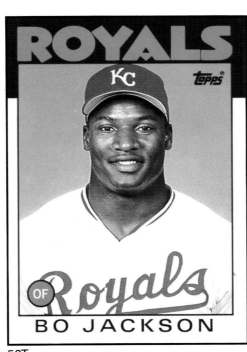

ROYALS

BO JACKSON

50T

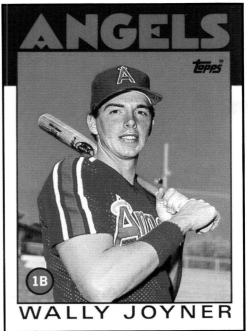

ANGELS

WALLY JOYNER

51T

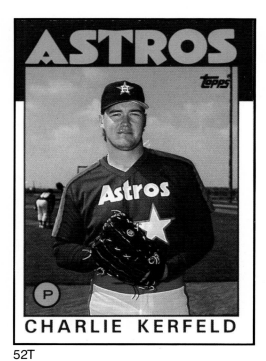

ASTROS

CHARLIE KERFELD

52T

TIGERS

ERIC KING

53T

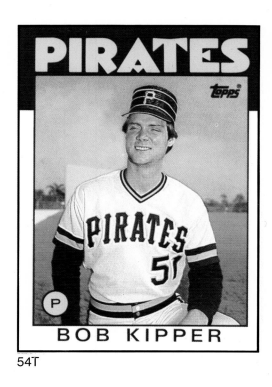

PIRATES

BOB KIPPER

54T

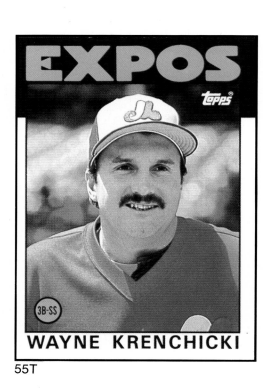

EXPOS

WAYNE KRENCHICKI

55T

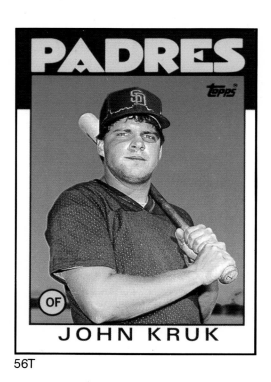

PADRES

JOHN KRUK

56T

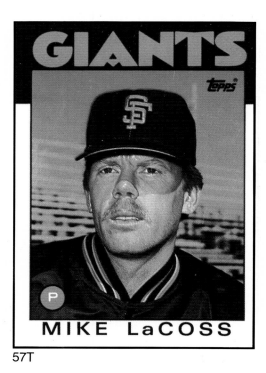

GIANTS

MIKE LaCOSS

57T

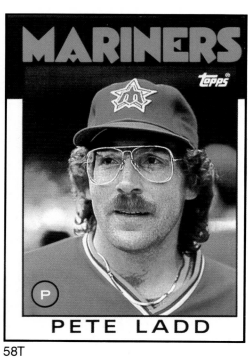

MARINERS

PETE LADD

58T

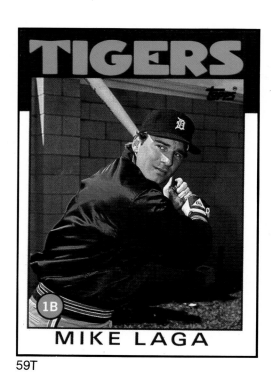

TIGERS

MIKE LAGA

59T

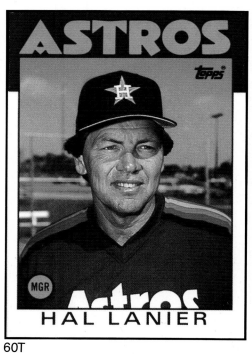

ASTROS

HAL LANIER

60T

TIGERS

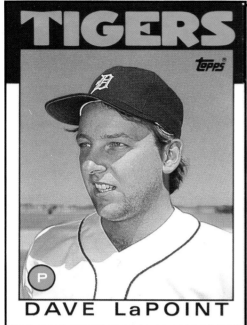

DAVE LaPOINT

61T

ROYALS

RUDY LAW

62T

BLUE JAYS

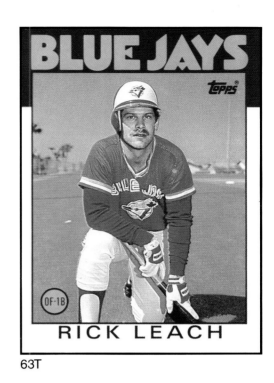

RICK LEACH

63T

BREWERS

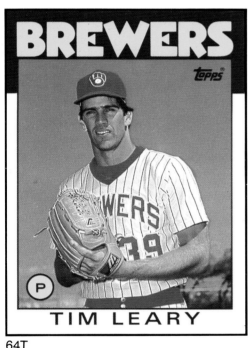

TIM LEARY

64T

ROYALS

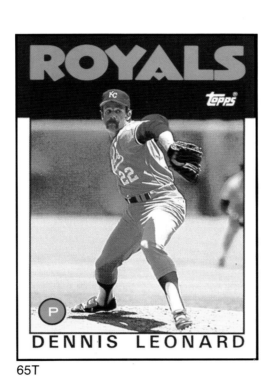

DENNIS LEONARD

65T

PIRATES

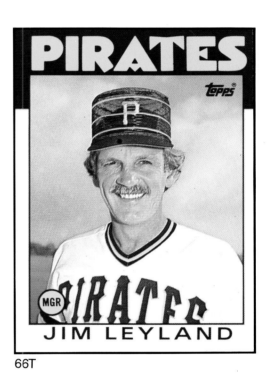

JIM LEYLAND

66T

WHITE SOX

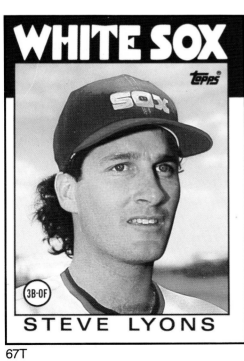

STEVE LYONS

67T

RANGERS

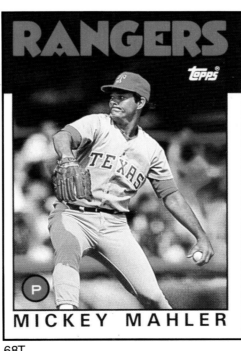

MICKEY MAHLER

68T

GIANTS

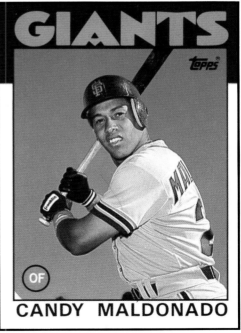

CANDY MALDONADO

69T

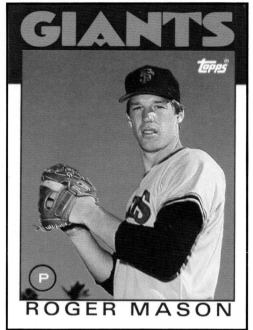

ROGER MASON

70T

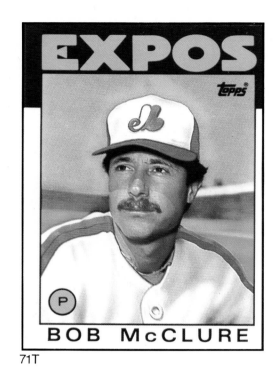

BOB McCLURE

71T

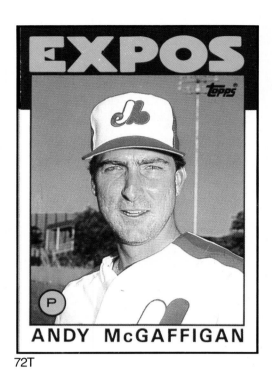

ANDY McGAFFIGAN

72T

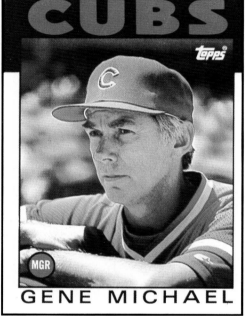

GENE MICHAEL

73T

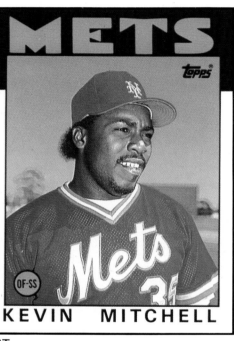

KEVIN MITCHELL

74T

OMAR MORENO

75T

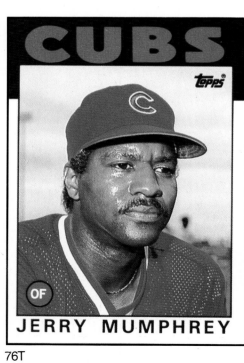

JERRY MUMPHREY

76T

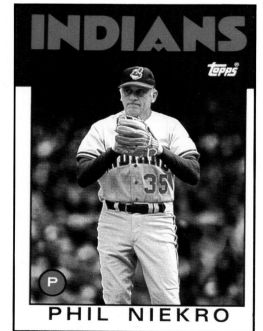

PHIL NIEKRO

77T

RANDY NIEMANN

78T

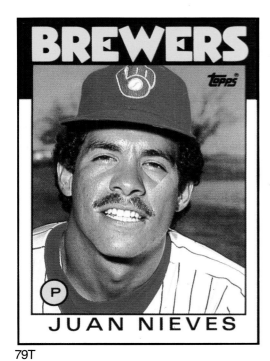

BREWERS

JUAN NIEVES

79T

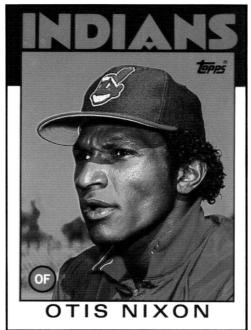

INDIANS

OTIS NIXON

80T

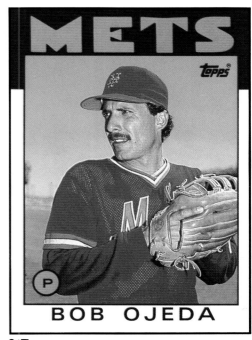

METS

BOB OJEDA

81T

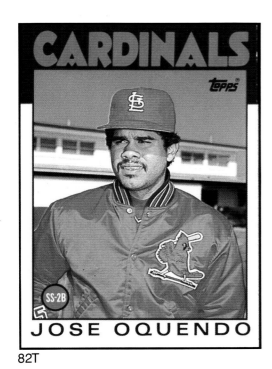

CARDINALS

JOSE OQUENDO

82T

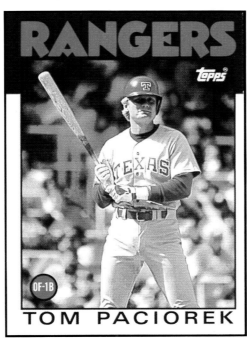

RANGERS

TOM PACIOREK

83T

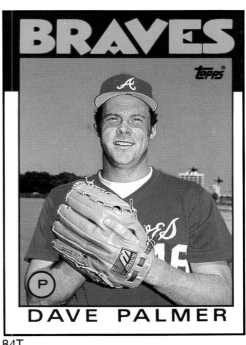

BRAVES

DAVE PALMER

84T

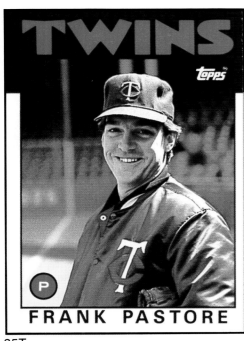

TWINS

FRANK PASTORE

85T

YANKEES

LOU PINIELLA

86T

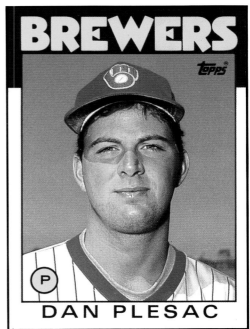

BREWERS

DAN PLESAC

87T

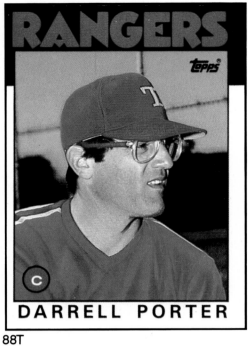

RANGERS

DARRELL PORTER

88T

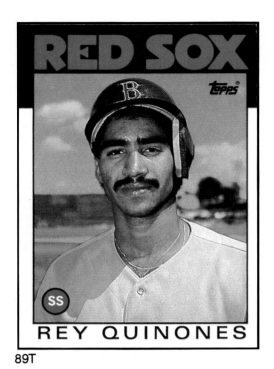

RED SOX

REY QUINONES

89T

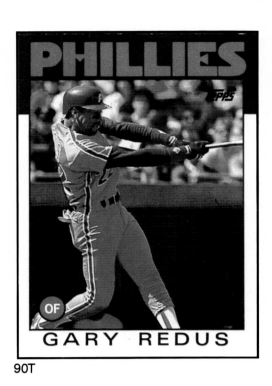

PHILLIES

GARY REDUS

90T

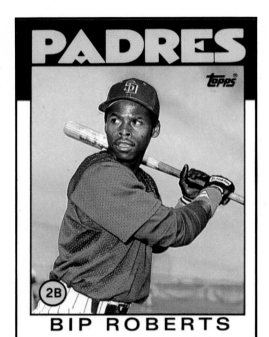

PADRES

BIP ROBERTS

91T

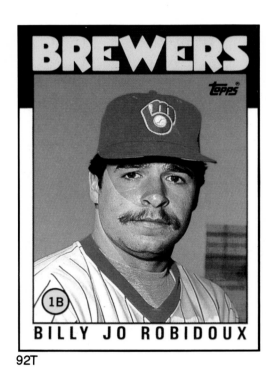

BREWERS

BILLY JO ROBIDOUX

92T

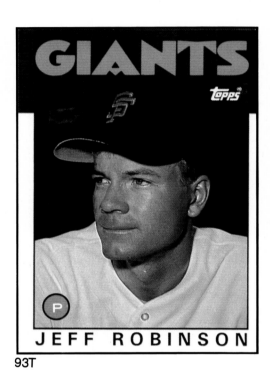

GIANTS

JEFF ROBINSON

93T

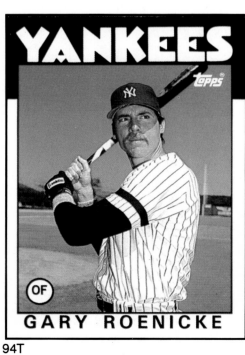

YANKEES

GARY ROENICKE

94T

RED SOX

ED ROMERO

95T

ROYALS

ARGENIS SALAZAR

96T

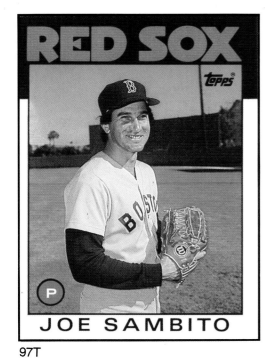

RED SOX

JOE SAMBITO

97T

BRAVES

BILLY SAMPLE

98T

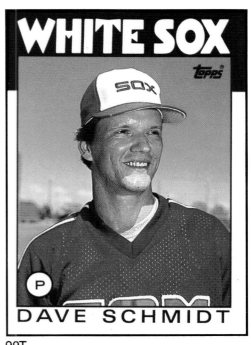

WHITE SOX

DAVE SCHMIDT

99T

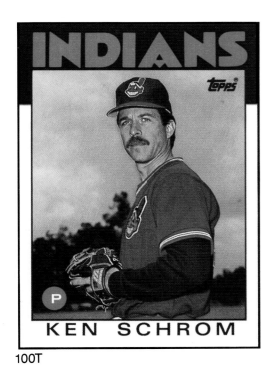

INDIANS

KEN SCHROM

100T

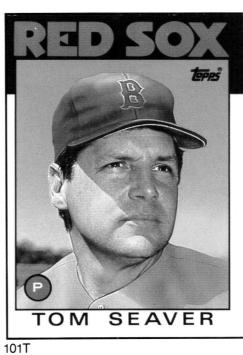

RED SOX

TOM SEAVER

101T

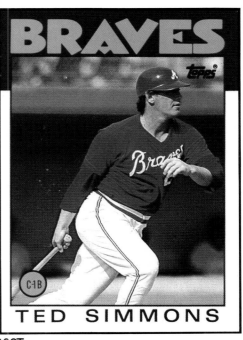

BRAVES

TED SIMMONS

102T

RED SOX

SAMMY STEWART

103T

REDS

KURT STILLWELL

104T

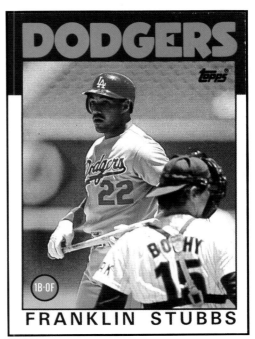

DODGERS

FRANKLIN STUBBS

105T

BREWERS

3B
DALE SVEUM
106T

BRAVES
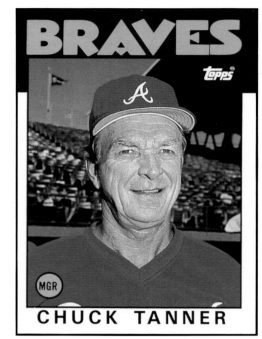
MGR
CHUCK TANNER
107T

MARINERS
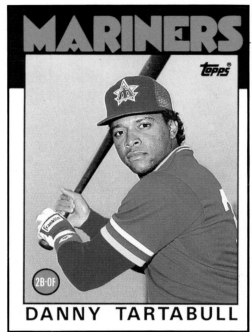
2B-OF
DANNY TARTABULL
108T

METS
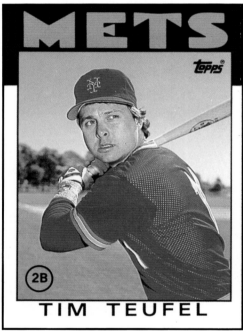
2B
TIM TEUFEL
109T

YANKEES
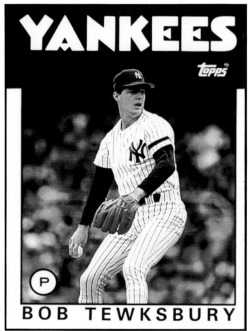
P
BOB TEWKSBURY
110T

BRAVES
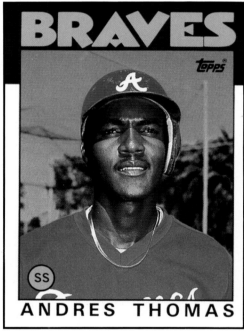
SS
ANDRES THOMAS
111T

PHILLIES
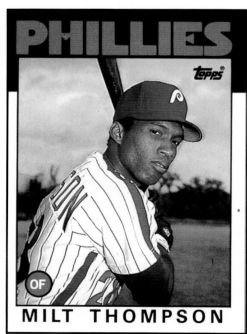
OF
MILT THOMPSON
112T

GIANTS

2B
ROBBY THOMPSON
113T

EXPOS

P
JAY TIBBS
114T

WHITE SOX
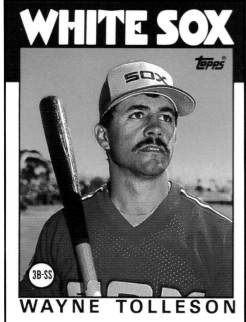
3B-SS
WAYNE TOLLESON
115T

DODGERS
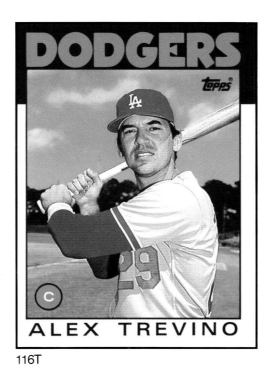
C
ALEX TREVINO
116T

CUBS
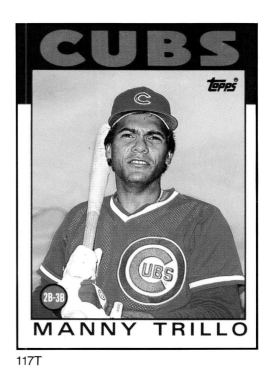
2B-3B
MANNY TRILLO
117T

DODGERS
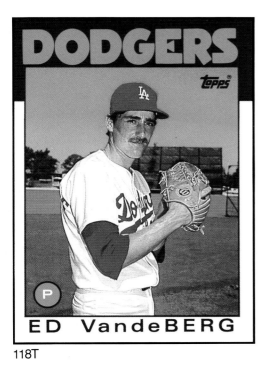
P
ED VandeBERG
118T

BRAVES
C
OZZIE VIRGIL
119T

PIRATES
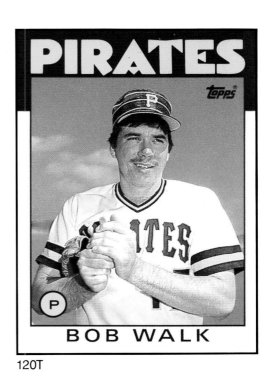
P
BOB WALK
120T

PADRES

P
GENE WALTER
121T

YANKEES
OF
CLAUDELL WASHINGTON
122T

BREWERS
P
BILL WEGMAN
123T

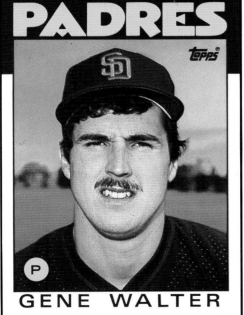

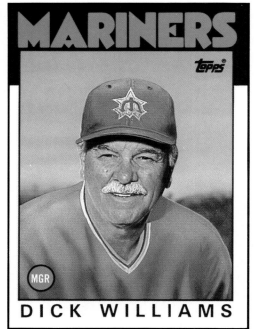

MARINERS

DICK WILLIAMS

124T

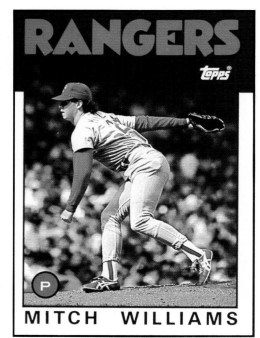

RANGERS

MITCH WILLIAMS

125T

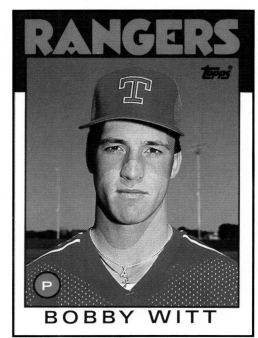

RANGERS

BOBBY WITT

126T

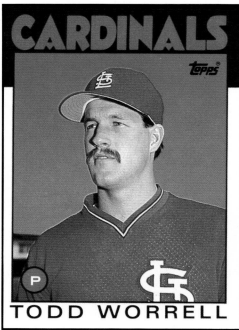

CARDINALS

TODD WORRELL

127T

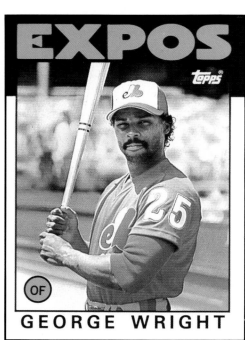

EXPOS

GEORGE WRIGHT

128T

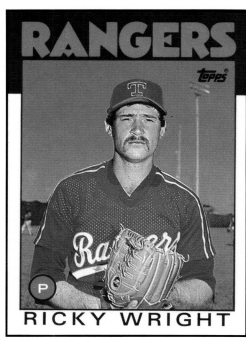

RANGERS

RICKY WRIGHT

129T

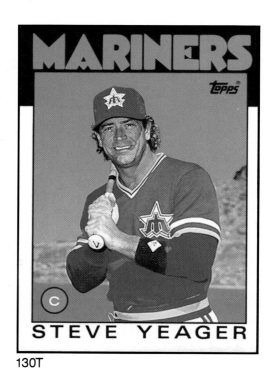

MARINERS

STEVE YEAGER

130T

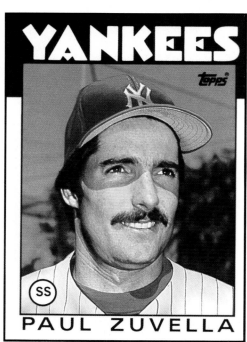

YANKEES

PAUL ZUVELLA

131T

1986 BASEBALL CHECKLIST   1T – 132T

1T ☐ ANDY ALLANSON	33T ☐ MIKE EASLER
2T ☐ NEIL ALLEN	34T ☐ MARK EICHHORN
3T ☐ JOAQUIN ANDUJAR	35T ☐ STEVE FARR
4T ☐ PAUL ASSENMACHER	36T ☐ SCOTT FLETCHER
5T ☐ SCOTT BAILES	37T ☐ TERRY FORSTER
6T ☐ DON BAYLOR	38T ☐ TERRY FRANCONA
7T ☐ STEVE BEDROSIAN	39T ☐ JIM FREGOSI
8T ☐ JUAN BENIQUEZ	40T ☐ ANDRES GALARRAGA
9T ☐ JUAN BERENGUER	41T ☐ KEN GRIFFEY
10T ☐ MIKE BIELECKI	42T ☐ BILL GULLICKSON
11T ☐ BARRY BONDS	43T ☐ JOSE GUZMAN
12T ☐ BOBBY BONILLA	44T ☐ MOOSE HAAS
13T ☐ JUAN BONILLA	45T ☐ BILLY HATCHER
14T ☐ RICH BORDI	46T ☐ MIKE HEATH
15T ☐ STEVE BOROS	47T ☐ TOM HUME
16T ☐ RICK BURLESON	48T ☐ PETE INCAVIGLIA
17T ☐ BILL CAMPBELL	49T ☐ DANE IORG
18T ☐ TOM CANDIOTTI	50T ☐ BO JACKSON
19T ☐ JOHN CANGELOSI	51T ☐ WALLY JOYNER
20T ☐ JOSE CANSECO	52T ☐ CHARLIE KERFELD
21T ☐ CARMEN CASTILLO	53T ☐ ERIC KING
22T ☐ RICK CERONE	54T ☐ BOB KIPPER
23T ☐ JOHN CERUTTI	55T ☐ WAYNE KRENCHICKI
24T ☐ WILL CLARK	56T ☐ JOHN KRUK
25T ☐ MARK CLEAR	57T ☐ MIKE LaCOSS
26T ☐ DARNELL COLES	58T ☐ PETE LADD
27T ☐ DAVE COLLINS	59T ☐ MIKE LAGA
28T ☐ TIM CONROY	60T ☐ HAL LANIER
29T ☐ JOE COWLEY	61T ☐ DAVE LaPOINT
30T ☐ JOEL DAVIS	62T ☐ RUDY LAW
31T ☐ ROB DEER	63T ☐ RICK LEACH
32T ☐ JOHN DENNY	64T ☐ TIM LEARY

132T

1987

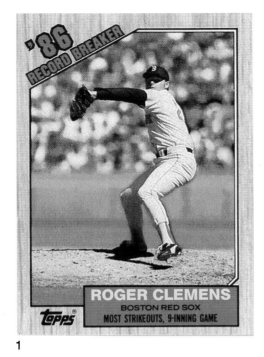

1

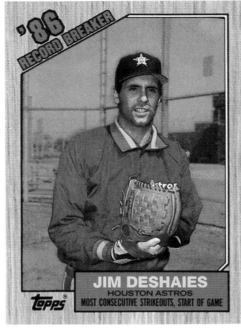

2

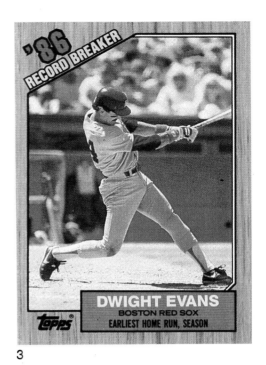

3

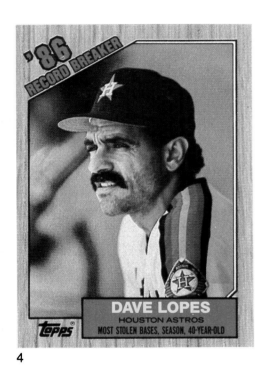

4

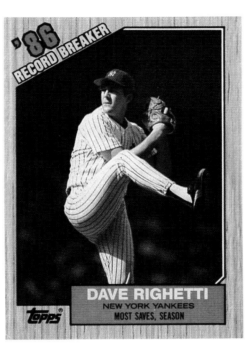

5

6

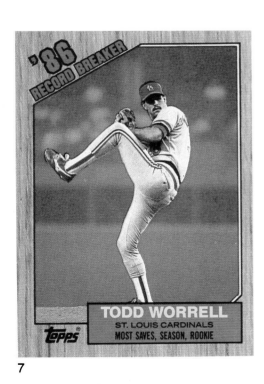

7

8

9

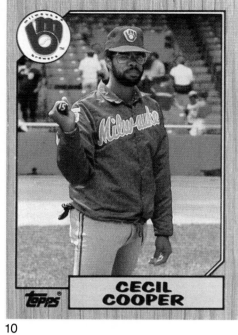

CECIL COOPER

10

INDIANS LEADERS

11

JEFF SELLERS

12

NICK ESASKY

13

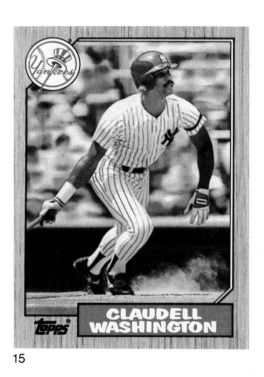

DAVE STEWART

14

CLAUDELL WASHINGTON

15

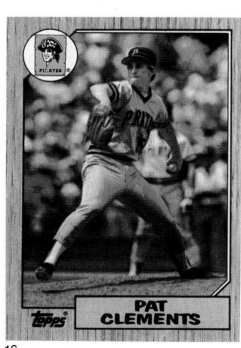

PAT CLEMENTS

16

PETE O'BRIEN

17

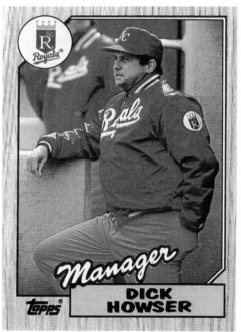

Manager

DICK HOWSER

18

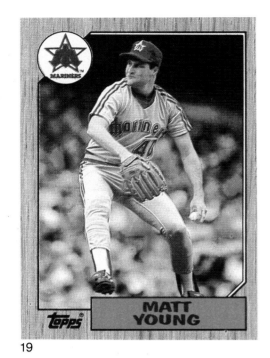

MATT YOUNG

19

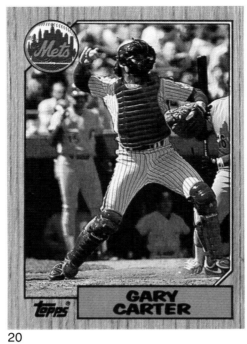

GARY CARTER

20

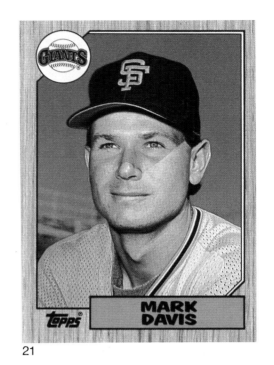

MARK DAVIS

21

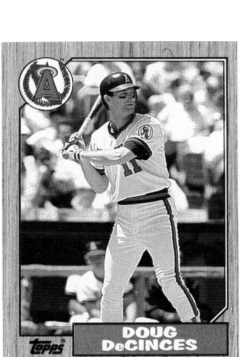

DOUG DeCINCES

22

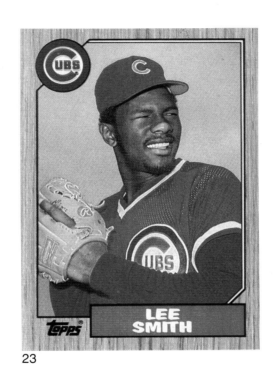

LEE SMITH

23

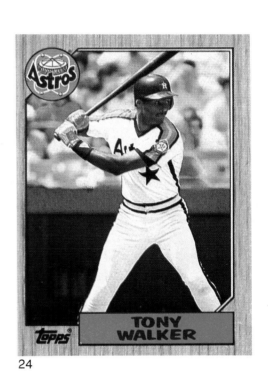

TONY WALKER

24

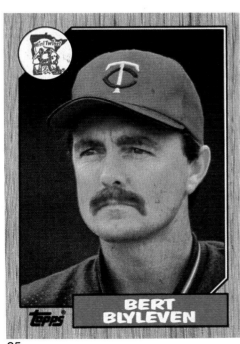

BERT BLYLEVEN

25

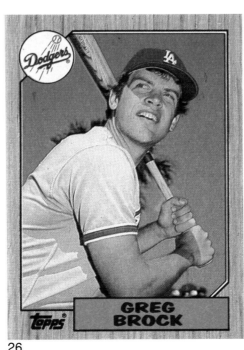

GREG BROCK

26

JOE COWLEY

27

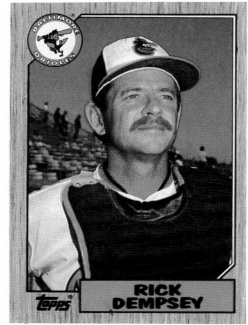

RICK DEMPSEY

28

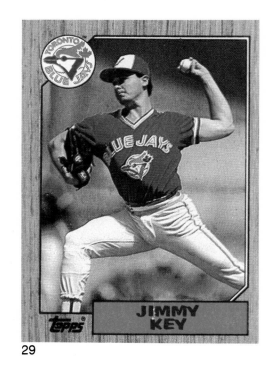

JIMMY KEY

29

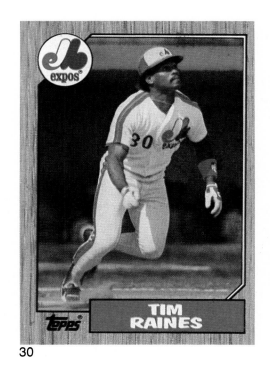

TIM RAINES

30

BRAVES LEADERS

31

TIM LEARY

32

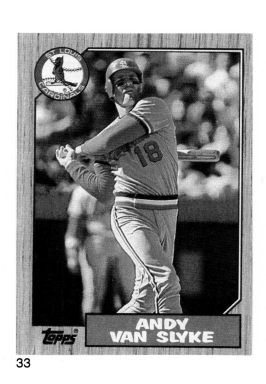

ANDY VAN SLYKE

33

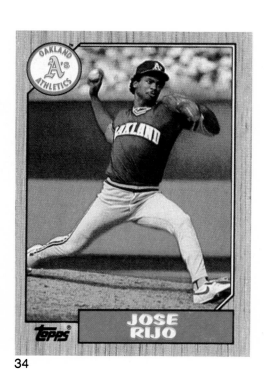

JOSE RIJO

34

SID BREAM

35

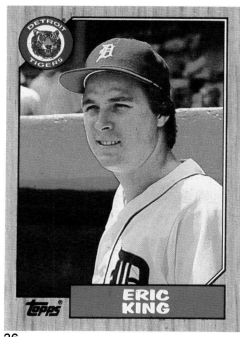

ERIC KING

36

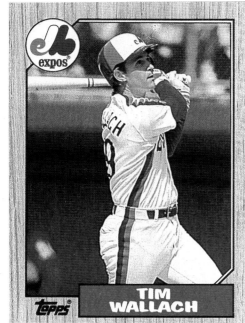

TIM WALLACH

55

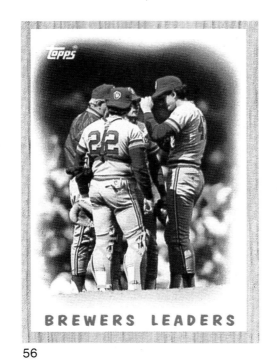

BREWERS LEADERS

56

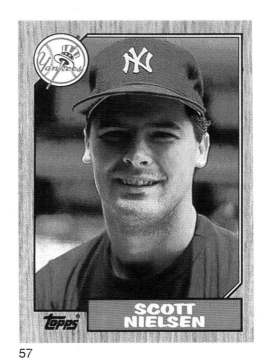

SCOTT NIELSEN

57

THAD BOSLEY

58

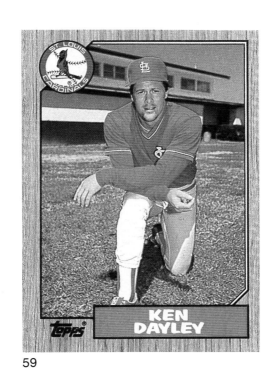

KEN DAYLEY

59

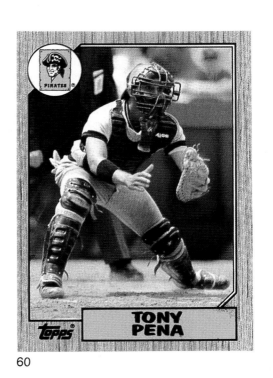

TONY PENA

60

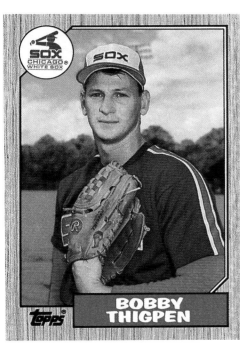

BOBBY THIGPEN

61

BOBBY MEACHAM

62

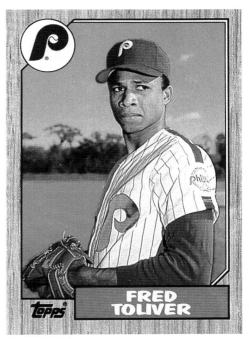

FRED TOLIVER

63

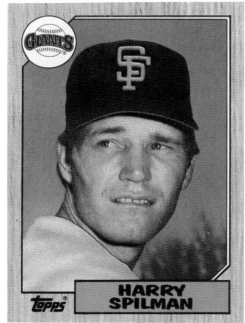

HARRY SPILMAN

64

TOM BROWNING

65

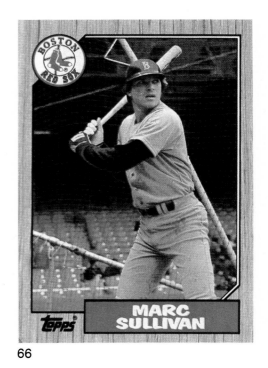

MARC SULLIVAN

66

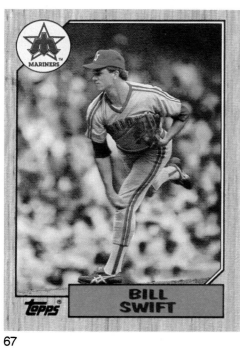

BILL SWIFT

67

TONY LaRUSSA

Manager

68

LONNIE SMITH

69

CHARLIE HOUGH

70

MIKE ALDRETE

71

WALT TERRELL

72

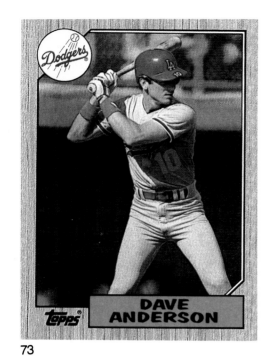

DAVE ANDERSON

73

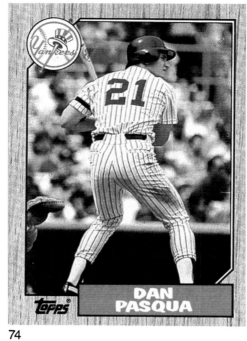

DAN PASQUA

74

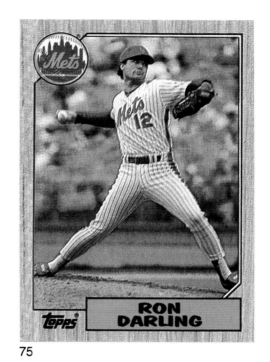

RON DARLING

75

RAFAEL RAMIREZ

76

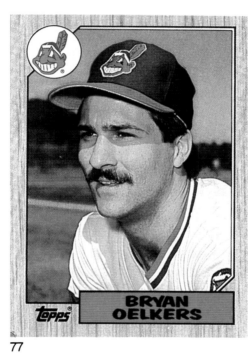

BRYAN OELKERS

77

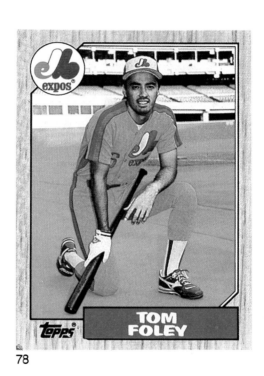

TOM FOLEY

78

JUAN NIEVES

79

WALLY JOYNER

80

PADRES LEADERS

81

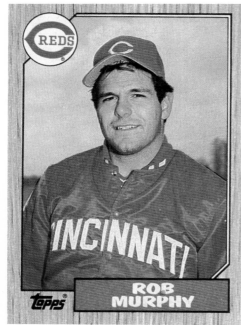

ROB MURPHY

82

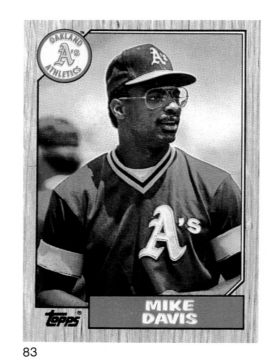

MIKE DAVIS

83

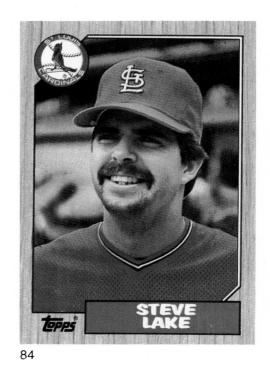

STEVE LAKE

84

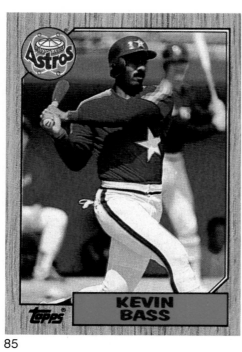

KEVIN BASS

85

NATE SNELL

86

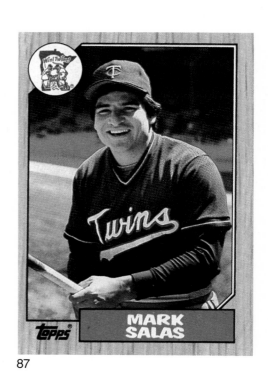

MARK SALAS

87

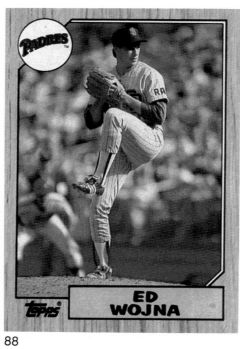

ED WOJNA

88

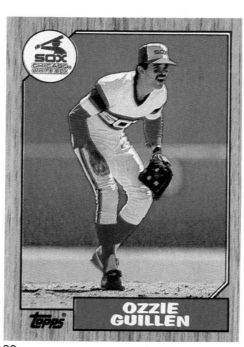

OZZIE GUILLEN

89

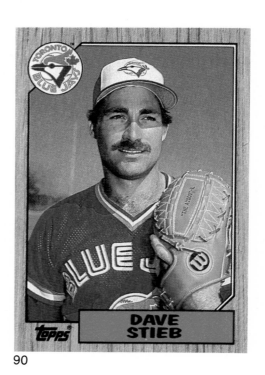

DAVE STIEB

90

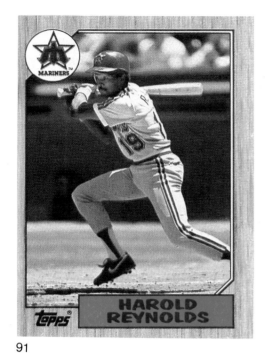

HAROLD REYNOLDS

91

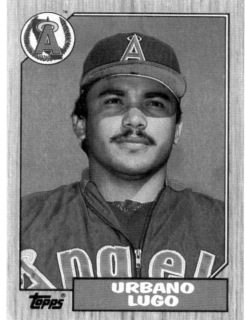

URBANO LUGO

92

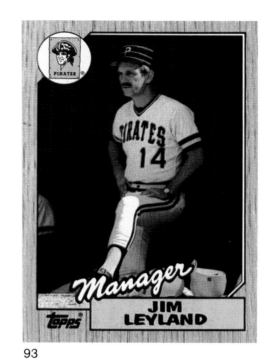

JIM LEYLAND

93

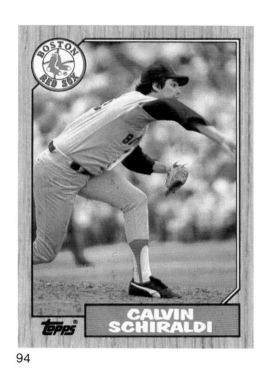

CALVIN SCHIRALDI

94

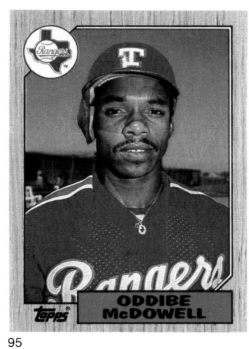

ODDIBE McDOWELL

95

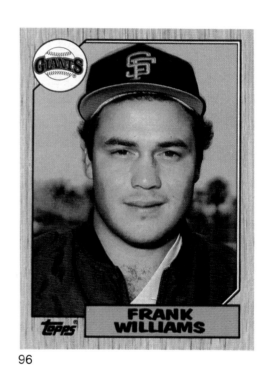

FRANK WILLIAMS

96

GLENN WILSON

97

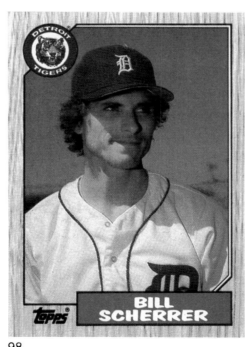

BILL SCHERRER

98

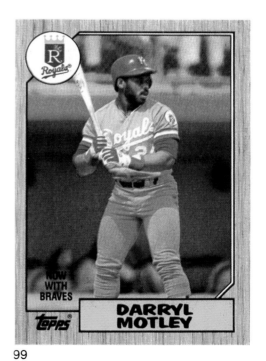

DARRYL MOTLEY

99

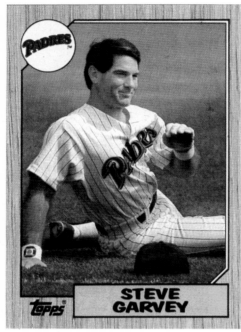

STEVE GARVEY

100

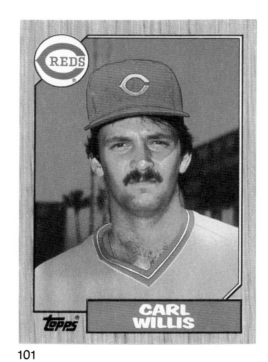

CARL WILLIS

101

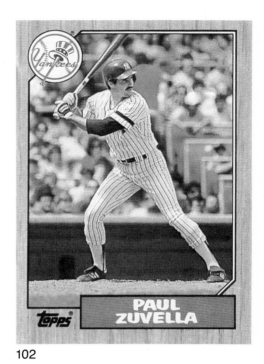

PAUL ZUVELLA

102

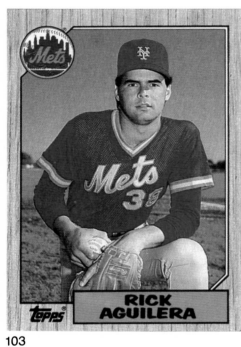

RICK AGUILERA

103

BILLY SAMPLE

104

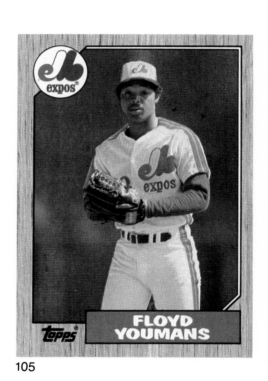

FLOYD YOUMANS

105

BLUE JAYS LEADERS

106

JOHN BUTCHER

107

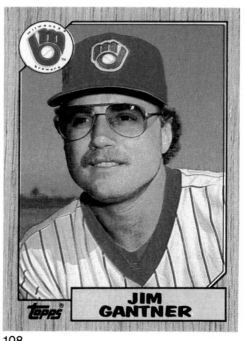

JIM GANTNER

108

R.J. REYNOLDS

109

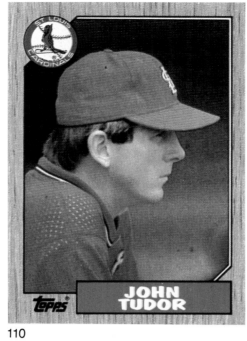

JOHN TUDOR

110

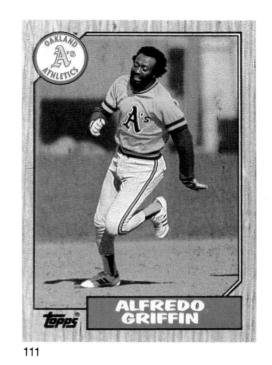

ALFREDO GRIFFIN

111

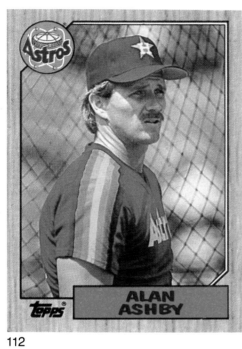

ALAN ASHBY

112

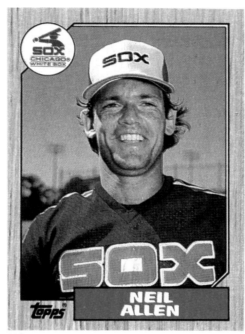

NEIL ALLEN

113

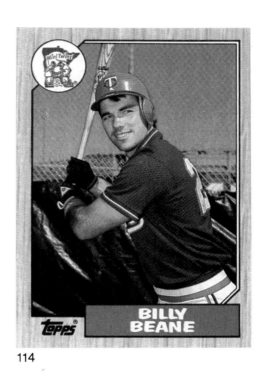

BILLY BEANE

114

DONNIE MOORE

115

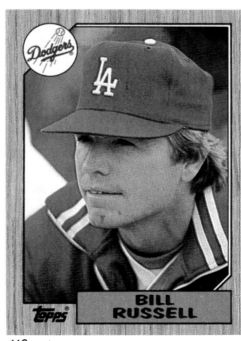

BILL RUSSELL

116

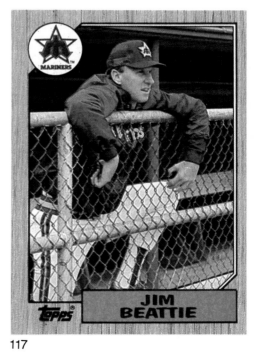

JIM BEATTIE

117

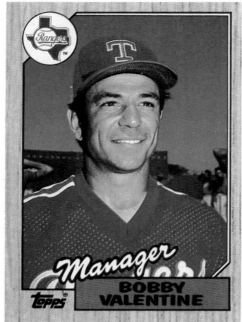

BOBBY
VALENTINE

118

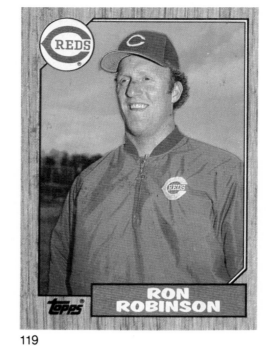

RON
ROBINSON

119

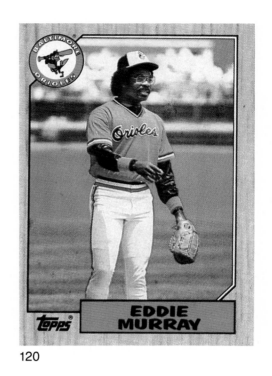

EDDIE
MURRAY

120

KEVIN
ROMINE

121

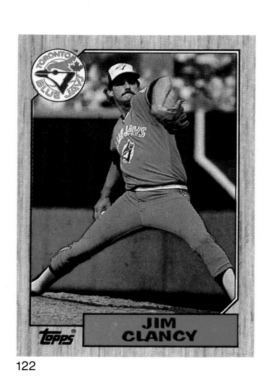

JIM
CLANCY

122

JOHN
KRUK

123

RAY
FONTENOT

124

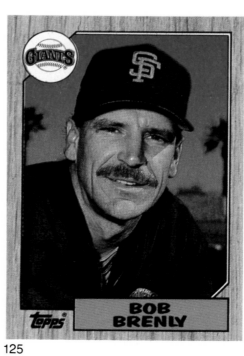

BOB
BRENLY

125

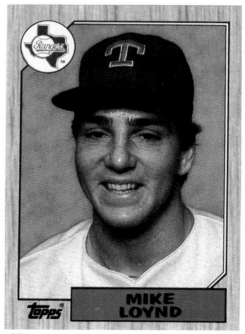

MIKE
LOYND

126

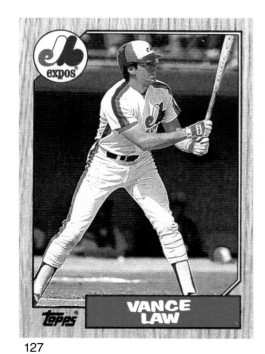

VANCE LAW

127

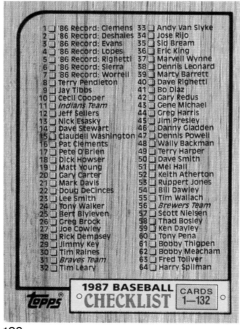

1987 BASEBALL CHECKLIST CARDS 1-132

128

RICK CERONE

129

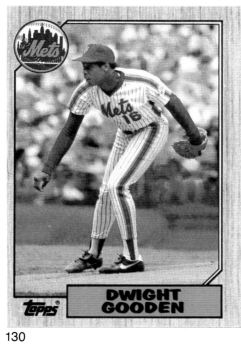

DWIGHT GOODEN

130

PIRATES LEADERS

131

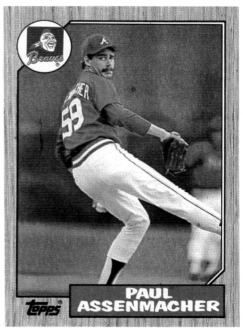

PAUL ASSENMACHER

132

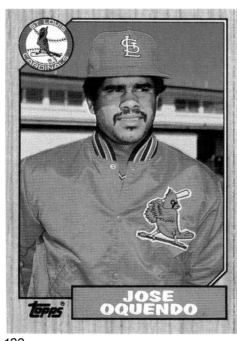

JOSE OQUENDO

133

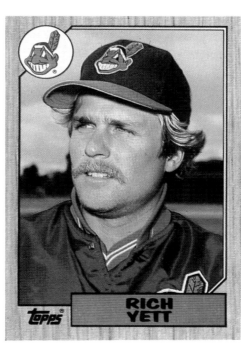

RICH YETT

134

MIKE EASLER

135

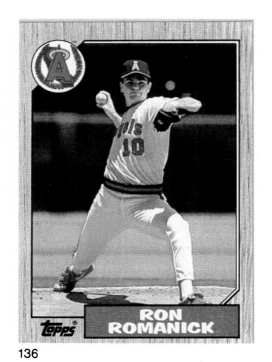

RON
ROMANICK

136

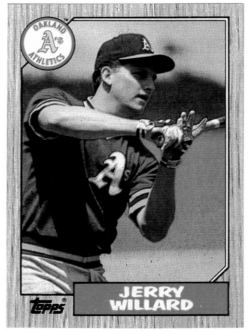

JERRY WILLARD

137

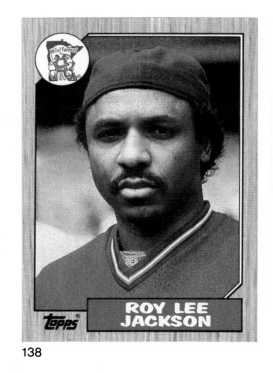

ROY LEE
JACKSON

138

DEVON
WHITE

139

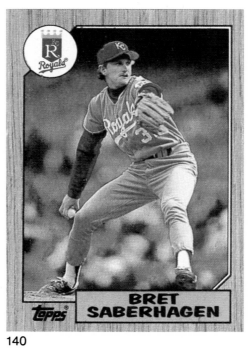

BRET
SABERHAGEN

140

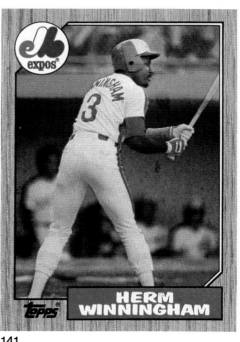

HERM
WINNINGHAM

141

RICK
SUTCLIFFE

142

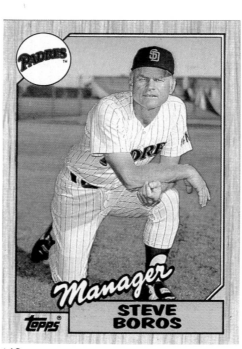

Manager
STEVE
BOROS

143

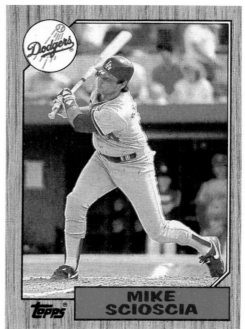

MIKE
SCIOSCIA

144

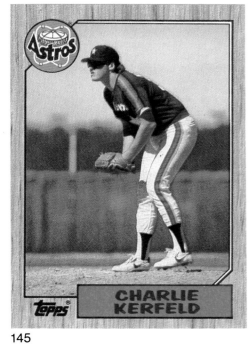

CHARLIE KERFELD

145

TRACY JONES

146

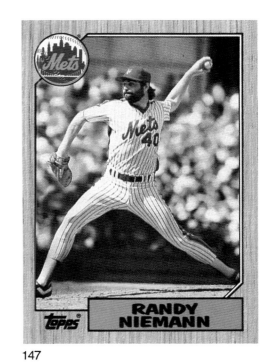

RANDY NIEMANN

147

DAVE COLLINS

148

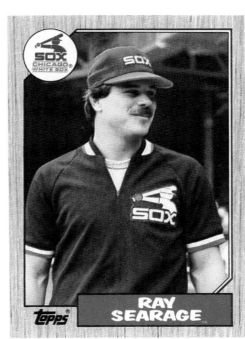

RAY SEARAGE

149

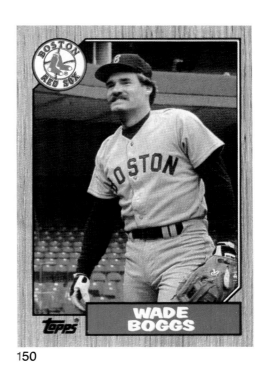

WADE BOGGS

150

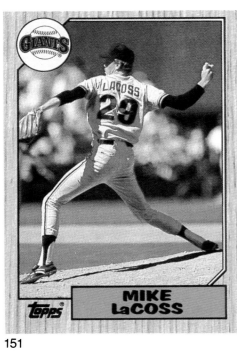

MIKE LaCOSS

151

TOBY HARRAH

152

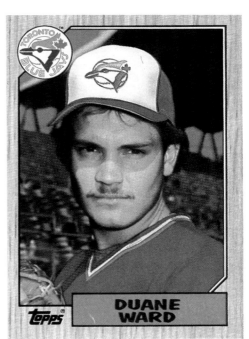

DUANE WARD

153

TOM
O'MALLEY

154

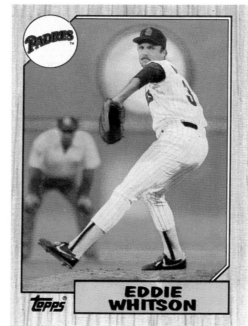

EDDIE
WHITSON

155

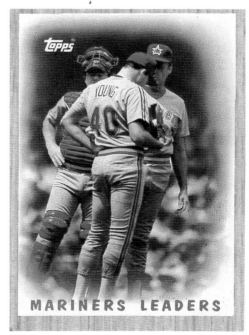

MARINERS LEADERS

156

DANNY
DARWIN

157

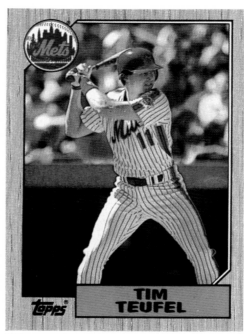

TIM
TEUFEL

158

ED
OLWINE

159

JULIO
FRANCO

160

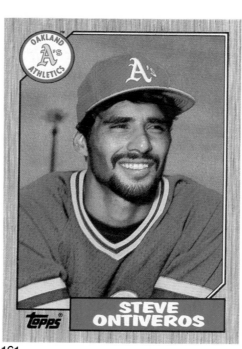

STEVE
ONTIVEROS

161

MIKE
LaVALLIERE

162

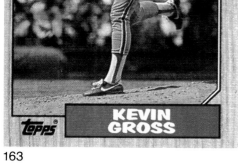

KEVIN GROSS

163

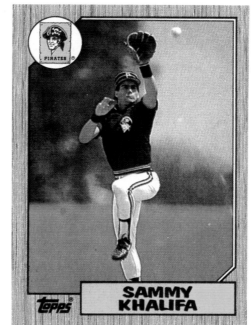

SAMMY KHALIFA

164

JEFF REARDON

165

BOB BOONE

166

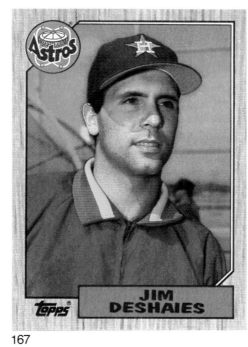

JIM DESHAIES

167

LOU PINIELLA

168

RON WASHINGTON

169

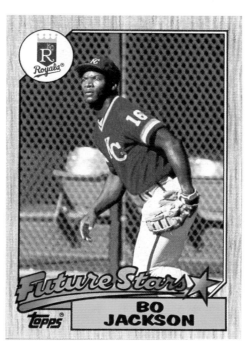

Future Stars

BO JACKSON

170

CHUCK CARY

171

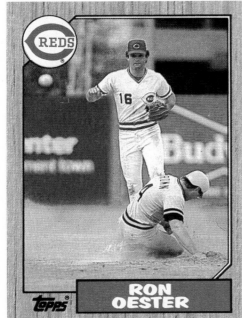

RON OESTER

172

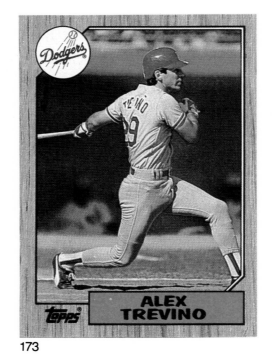

ALEX TREVINO

173

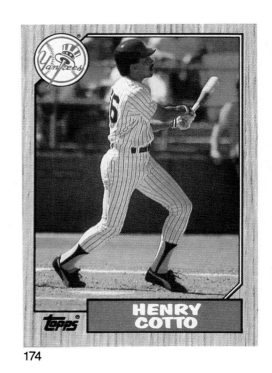

HENRY COTTO

174

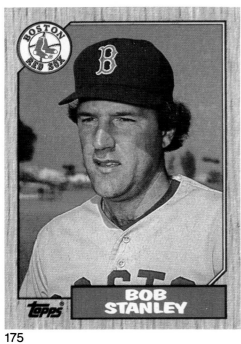

BOB STANLEY

175

STEVE BUECHELE

176

KEITH MORELAND

177

CECIL FIELDER

178

BILL WEGMAN

179

CHRIS BROWN

180

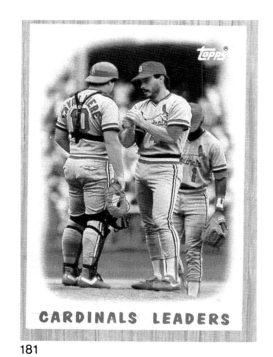

CARDINALS LEADERS

181

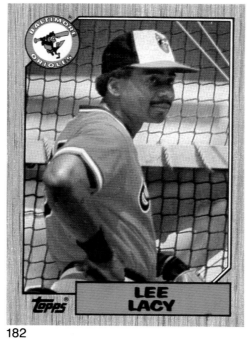

LEE LACY

182

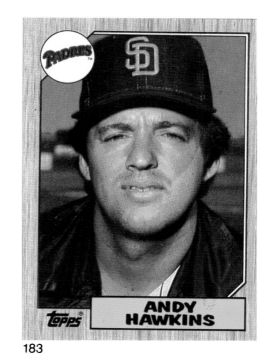

ANDY HAWKINS

183

BOBBY BONILLA

184

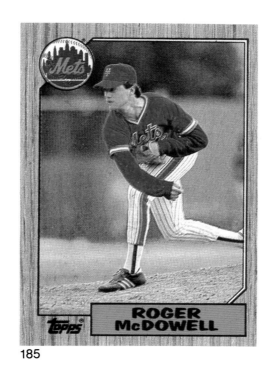

ROGER McDOWELL

185

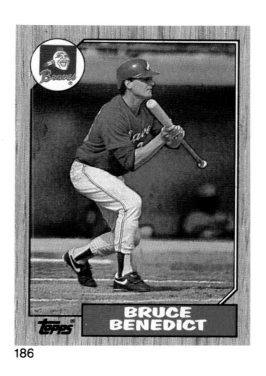

BRUCE BENEDICT

186

MARK HUISMANN

187

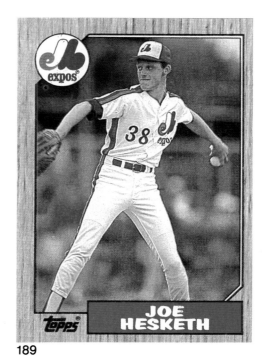

TONY PHILLIPS

188

JOE HESKETH

189

JIM SUNDBERG

190

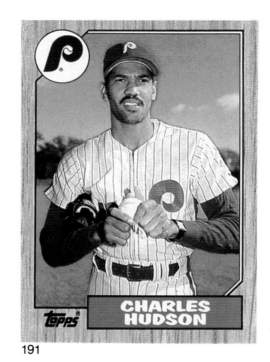

CHARLES HUDSON

191

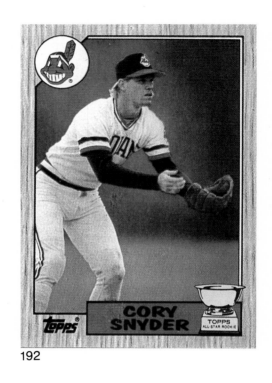

CORY SNYDER

192

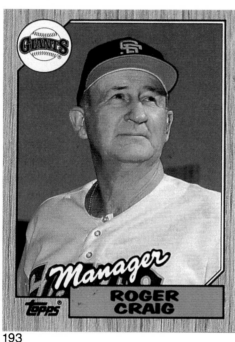

ROGER CRAIG

193

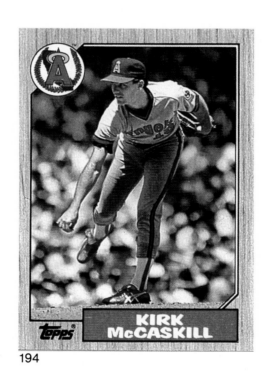

KIRK McCASKILL

194

MIKE PAGLIARULO

195

RANDY O'NEAL

196

MARK BAILEY

197

LEE MAZZILLI

198

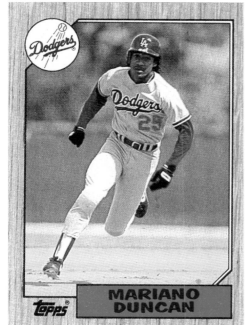

MARIANO DUNCAN

199

PETE ROSE

200

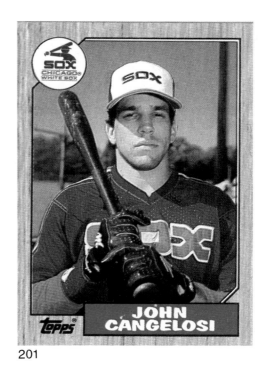

JOHN CANGELOSI

201

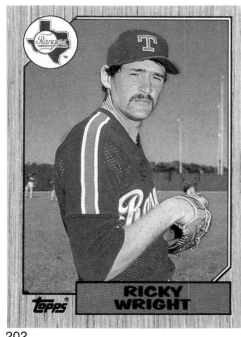

RICKY WRIGHT

202

MIKE KINGERY

203

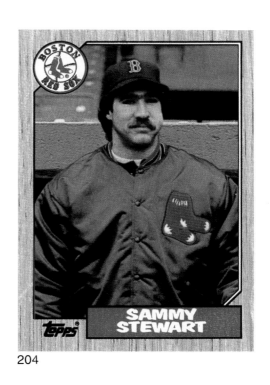

SAMMY STEWART

204

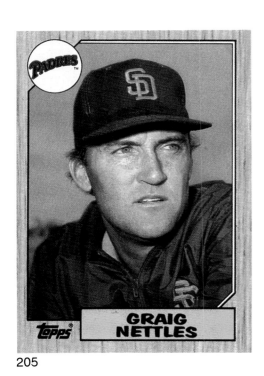

GRAIG NETTLES

205

TWINS LEADERS

206

GEORGE FRAZIER

207

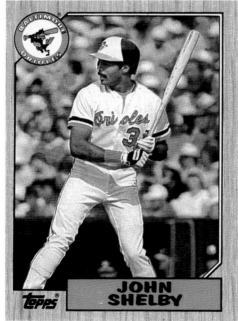

JOHN
SHELBY

208

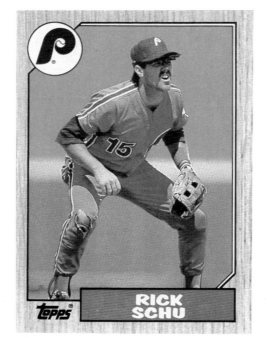

RICK
SCHU

209

LLOYD
MOSEBY

210

JOHN
MORRIS

211

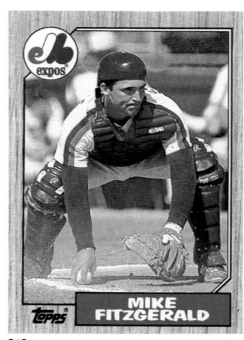

MIKE
FITZGERALD

212

RANDY
MYERS

213

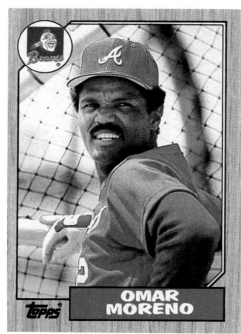

OMAR
MORENO

214

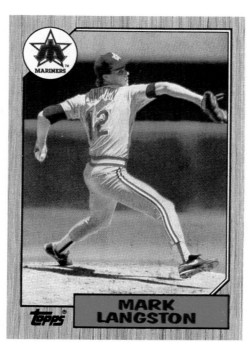

MARK
LANGSTON

215

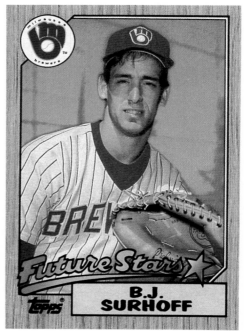

B.J.
SURHOFF

216

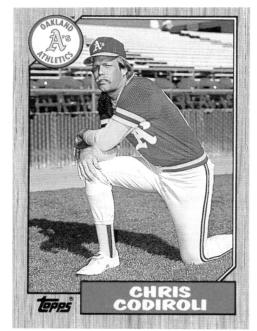

CHRIS
CODIROLI

217

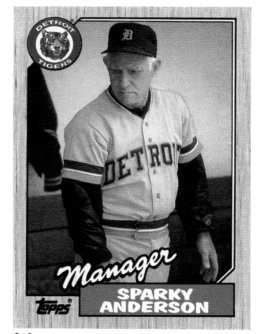

Manager

SPARKY
ANDERSON

218

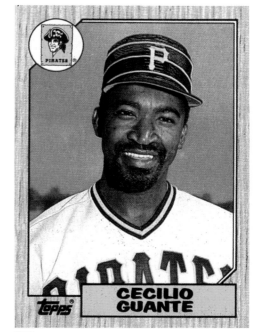

CECILIO
GUANTE

219

JOE
CARTER

220

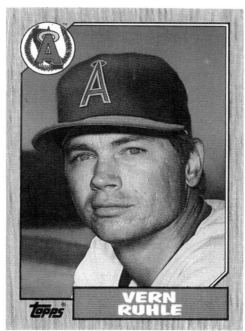

VERN
RUHLE

221

DENNY
WALLING

222

CHARLIE
LEIBRANDT

223

WAYNE
TOLLESON

224

MIKE
SMITHSON

225

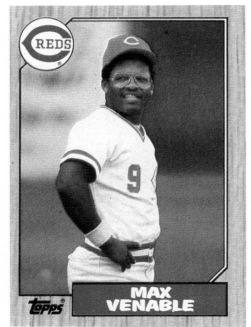

MAX VENABLE

226

JAMIE MOYER

227

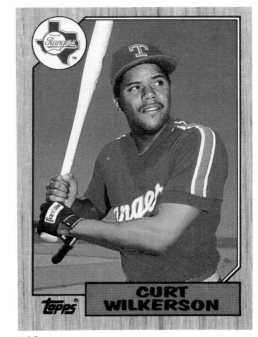

CURT WILKERSON

228

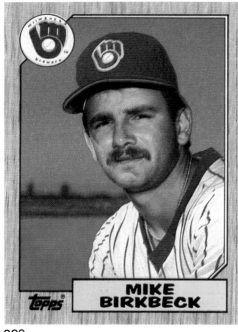

MIKE BIRKBECK

229

DON BAYLOR

230

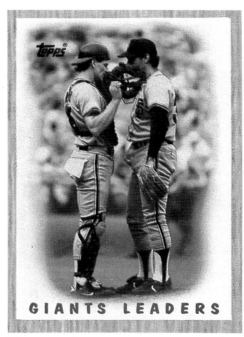

GIANTS LEADERS

231

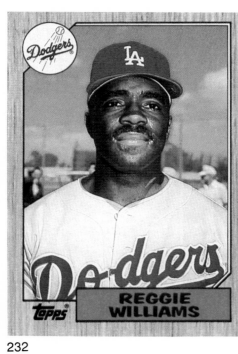

REGGIE WILLIAMS

232

RUSS MORMAN

233

PAT SHERIDAN

234

ALVIN
DAVIS

235

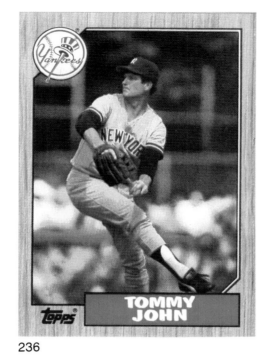

TOMMY
JOHN

236

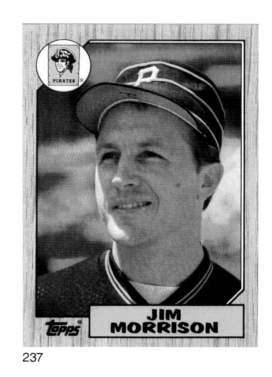

JIM
MORRISON

237

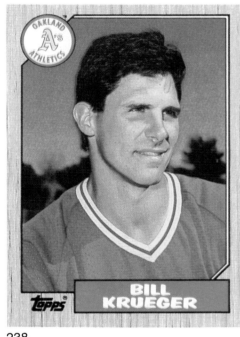

BILL
KRUEGER

238

JUAN
ESPINO

239

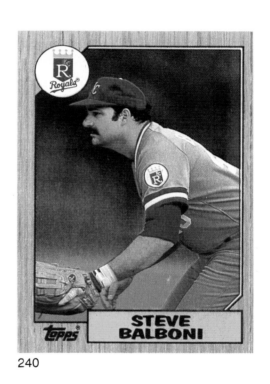

STEVE
BALBONI

240

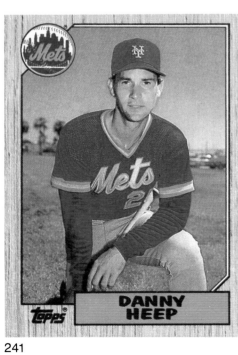

DANNY
HEEP

241

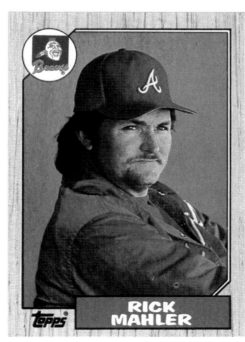

RICK
MAHLER

242

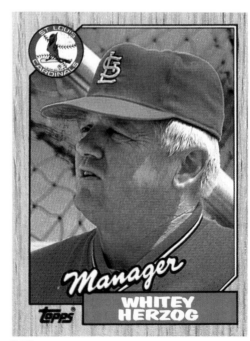

WHITEY
HERZOG

243

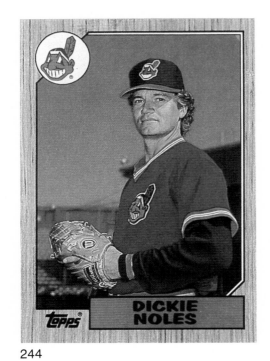

DICKIE NOLES

244

WILLIE UPSHAW

245

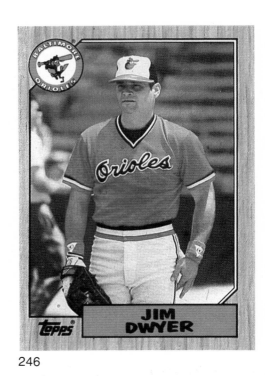

JIM DWYER

246

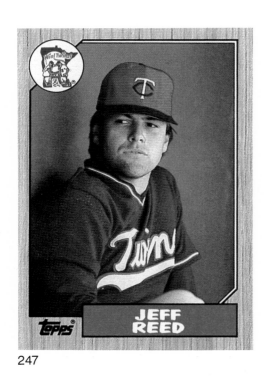

JEFF REED

247

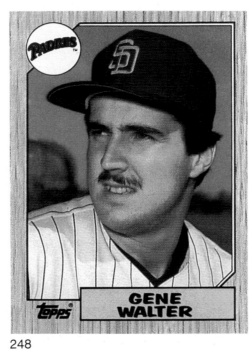

GENE WALTER

248

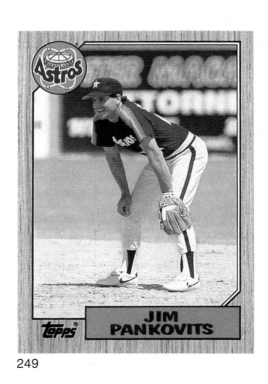

JIM PANKOVITS

249

TEDDY HIGUERA

250

ROB WILFONG

251

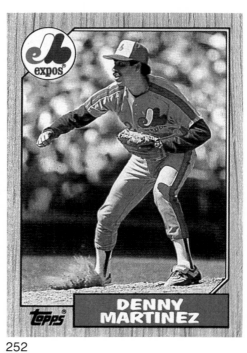

DENNY MARTINEZ

252

EDDIE MILNER

253

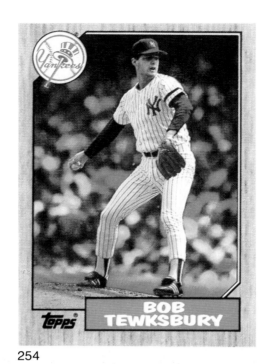

BOB TEWKSBURY

254

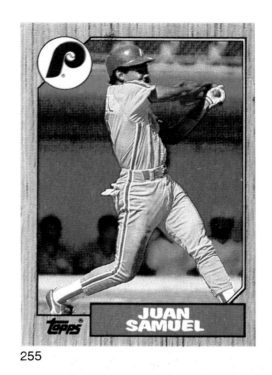

JUAN SAMUEL

255

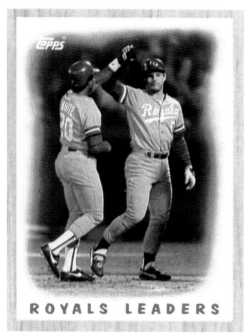

ROYALS LEADERS

256

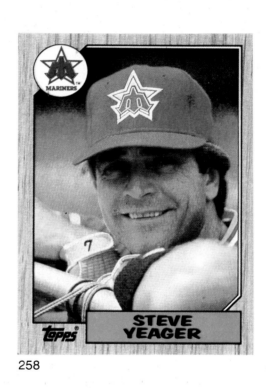

BOB FORSCH

257

STEVE YEAGER

258

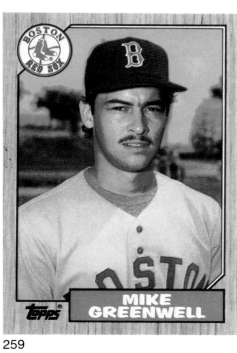

MIKE GREENWELL

259

VIDA BLUE

260

RUBEN SIERRA

261

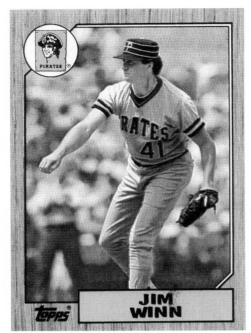

262

JIM WINN

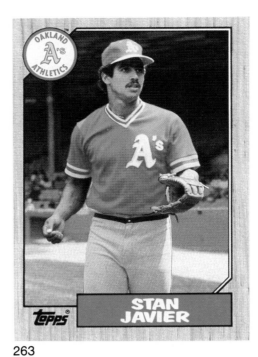

263

STAN JAVIER

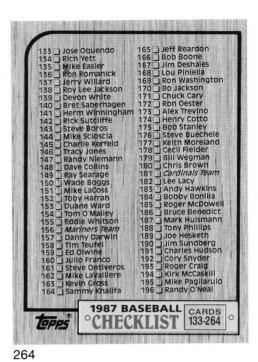

264

133	Jose Oquendo	165	Jeff Reardon
134	Rich Yett	166	Bob Boone
135	Mike Easler	167	Jim Deshaies
136	Ron Romanick	168	Lou Piniella
137	Jerry Willard	169	Ron Washington
138	Roy Lee Jackson	170	Bo Jackson
139	Devon White	171	Chuck Cary
140	Bret Saberhagen	172	Ron Oester
141	Herm Winningham	173	Alex Trevino
142	Rick Sutcliffe	174	Henry Cotto
143	Steve Boros	175	Bob Stanley
144	Mike Scioscia	176	Steve Buechele
145	Charlie Kerfeld	177	Keith Moreland
146	Tracy Jones	178	Cecil Fielder
147	Randy Niemann	179	Bill Wegman
148	Dave Collins	180	Chris Brown
149	Ray Searage	181	Cardinals Team
150	Wade Boggs	182	Lee Lacy
151	Mike LaCoss	183	Andy Hawkins
152	Toby Harrah	184	Bobby Bonilla
153	Duane Ward	185	Roger McDowell
154	Tom O'Malley	186	Bruce Benedict
155	Eddie Whitson	187	Mark Huismann
156	Mariners Team	188	Tony Phillips
157	Danny Darwin	189	Joe Hesketh
158	Tim Teufel	190	Jim Sundberg
159	Ed Olwine	191	Charles Hudson
160	Julio Franco	192	Cory Snyder
161	Steve Ontiveros	193	Roger Craig
162	Mike LaValliere	194	Kirk McCaskill
163	Kevin Gross	195	Mike Pagliarulo
164	Sammy Khalifa	196	Randy O'Neal

1987 BASEBALL CHECKLIST CARDS 133-264

265

DARRELL EVANS

266

JEFF HAMILTON

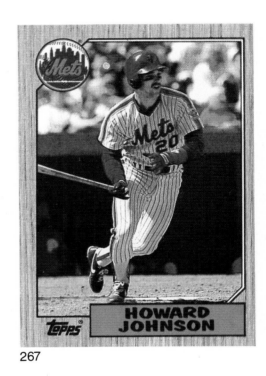

267

HOWARD JOHNSON

268

Manager PAT CORRALES

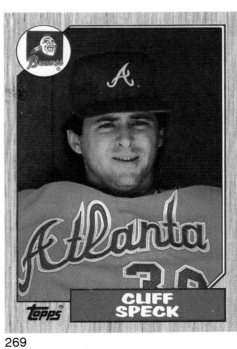

269

CLIFF SPECK

270

JODY DAVIS

MIKE BROWN

271

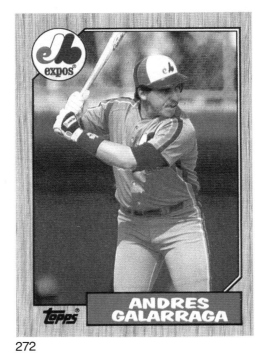

ANDRES GALARRAGA

272

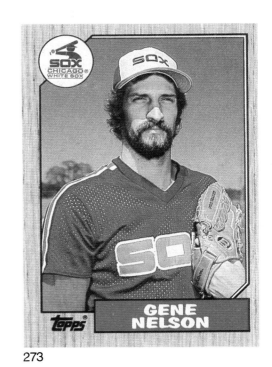

GENE NELSON

273

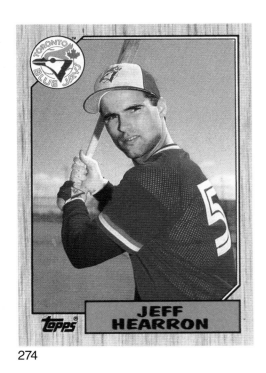

JEFF HEARRON

274

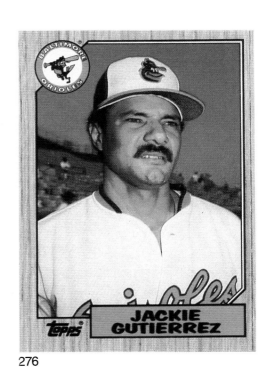

LaMARR HOYT

275

JACKIE GUTIERREZ

276

JUAN AGOSTO

277

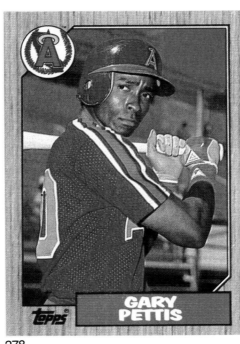

GARY PETTIS

278

DAN PLESAC

279

JEFFREY LEONARD

280

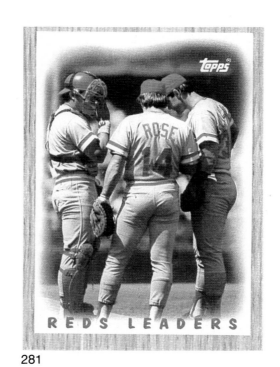

REDS LEADERS

281

JEFF CALHOUN

282

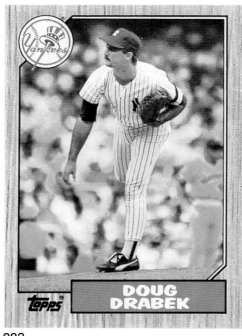

DOUG DRABEK

283

JOHN MOSES

284

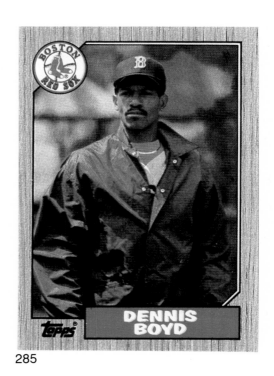

DENNIS BOYD

285

MIKE WOODARD

286

DAVE VON OHLEN

287

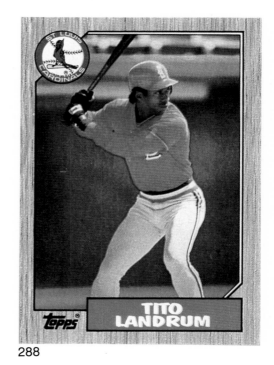

TITO LANDRUM

288

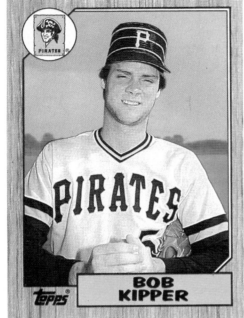

BOB
KIPPER

289

LEON DURHAM

290

MITCH
WILLIAMS

291

FRANKLIN
STUBBS

292

BOB
RODGERS

293

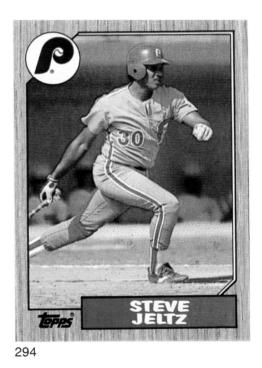

STEVE
JELTZ

294

LEN
DYKSTRA

295

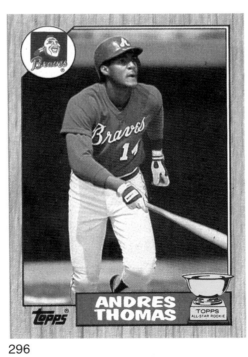

ANDRES
THOMAS

296

DON
SCHULZE

297

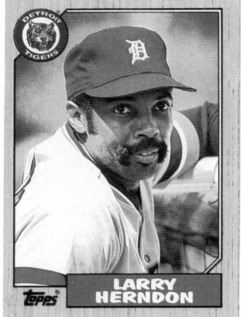

LARRY
HERNDON

298

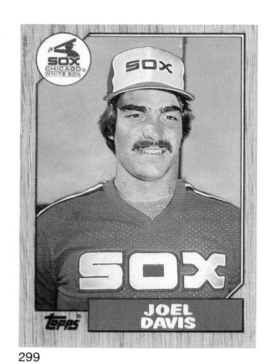

JOEL
DAVIS

299

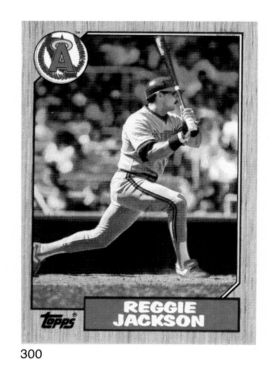

REGGIE
JACKSON

300

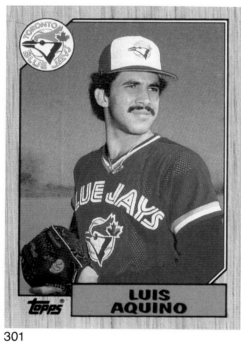

LUIS
AQUINO

301

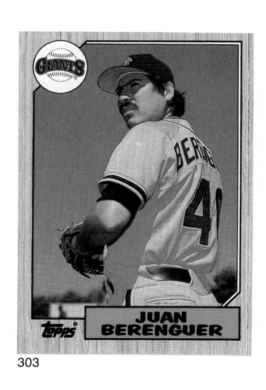

BILL
SCHROEDER

302

JUAN
BERENGUER

303

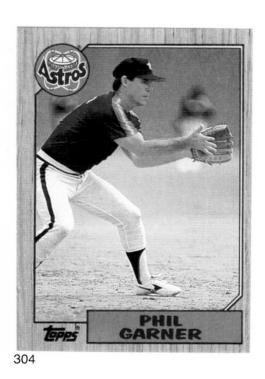

PHIL
GARNER

304

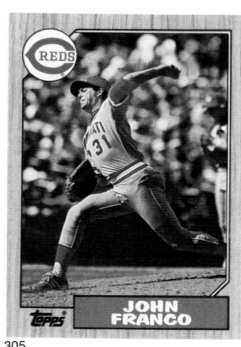

JOHN
FRANCO

305

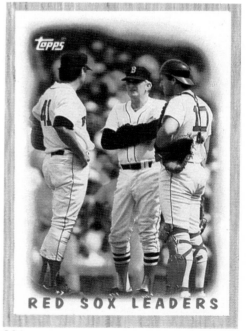

RED SOX LEADERS

306

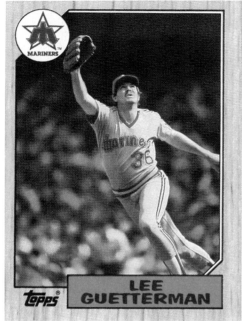

LEE GUETTERMAN

307

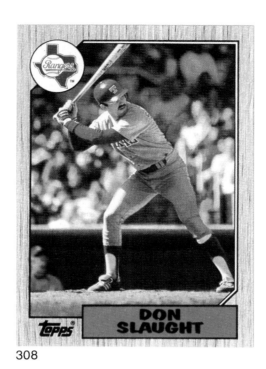

DON SLAUGHT

308

MIKE YOUNG

309

FRANK VIOLA

310

TURN BACK THE CLOCK

A'S
OUTFIELD RICKEY HENDERSON

1982

311

TURN BACK THE CLOCK

YANKEES
REGGIE JACKSON OUTFIELD

1977

312

TURN BACK THE CLOCK

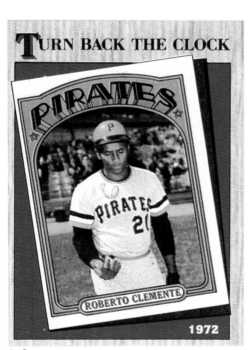

PIRATES

ROBERTO CLEMENTE

1972

313

TURN BACK THE CLOCK

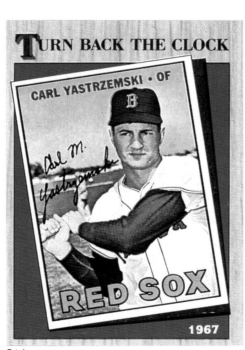

CARL YASTRZEMSKI • OF

RED SOX

1967

314

TURN BACK THE CLOCK

MAURY WILLS
L.A. DODGERS SS

1962

315

BRIAN
FISHER

316

CLINT HURDLE

317

JIM
FREGOSI

318

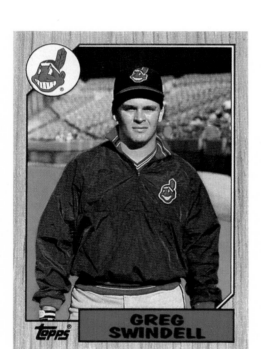

GREG
SWINDELL

319

BARRY
BONDS

320

MIKE
LAGA

321

CHRIS
BANDO

322

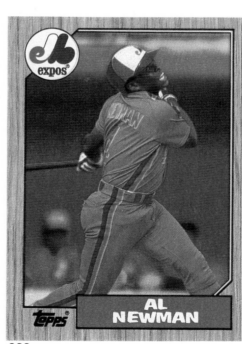

AL
NEWMAN

323

DAVE PALMER

324

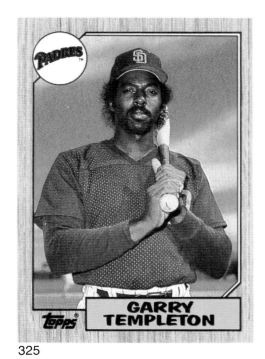

GARRY TEMPLETON

325

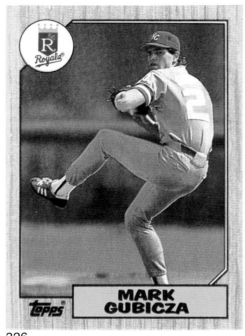

MARK GUBICZA

326

DALE SVEUM

327

BOB WELCH

328

RON ROENICKE

329

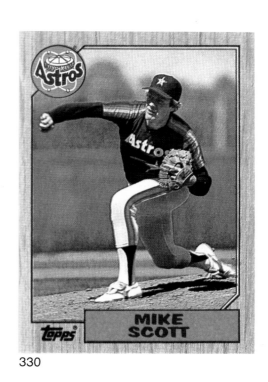

MIKE SCOTT

330

METS LEADERS

331

JOE PRICE

332

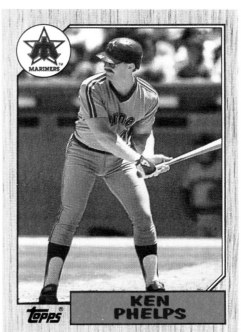

KEN PHELPS

333

ED
CORREA

334

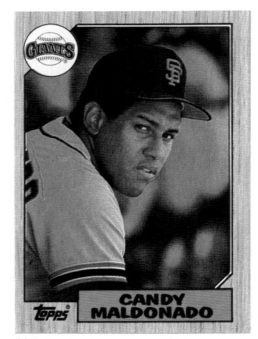

CANDY
MALDONADO

335

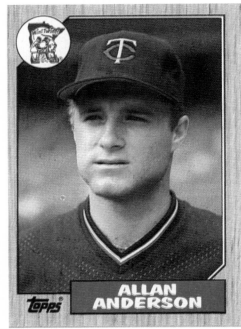

ALLAN
ANDERSON

336

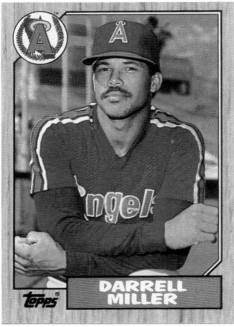

DARRELL
MILLER

337

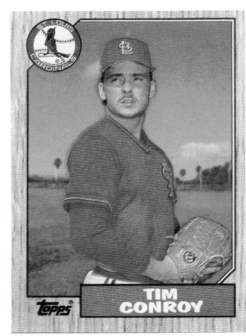

TIM
CONROY

338

DONNIE
HILL

339

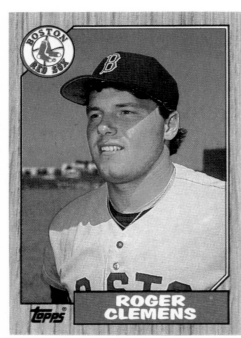

ROGER
CLEMENS

340

MIKE
BROWN

341

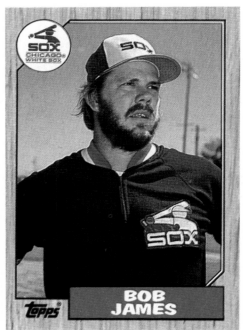

BOB
JAMES

342

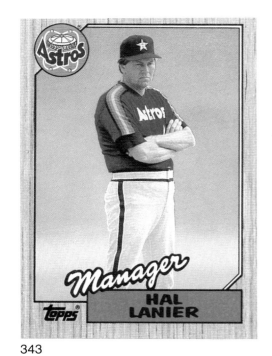

HAL LANIER

343

JOE NIEKRO

344

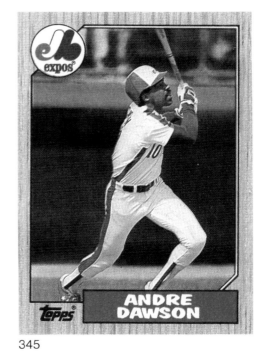

ANDRE DAWSON

345

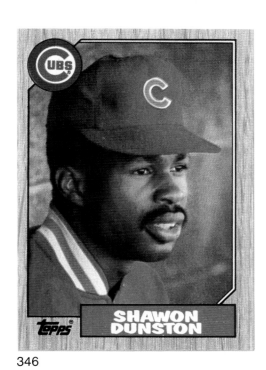

SHAWON DUNSTON

346

MICKEY BRANTLEY

347

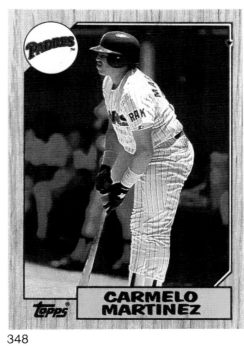

CARMELO MARTINEZ

348

STORM DAVIS

349

KEITH HERNANDEZ

350

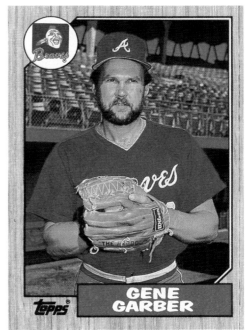

GENE GARBER

351

MIKE FELDER

352

ERNIE CAMACHO

353

JAMIE QUIRK

354

DON CARMAN

355

WHITE SOX LEADERS

356

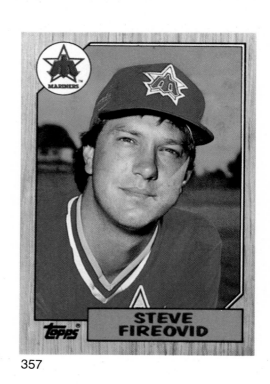

STEVE FIREOVID

357

SAL BUTERA

358

DOUG CORBETT

359

PEDRO GUERRERO

360

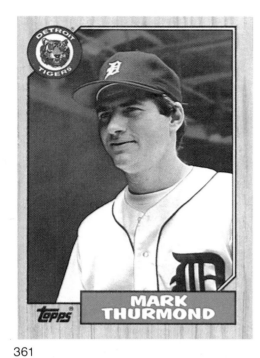

MARK THURMOND

361

LUIS QUINONES

362

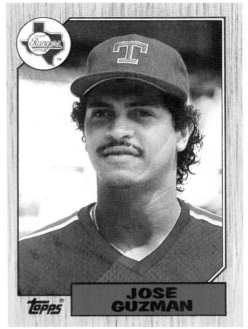

JOSE GUZMAN

363

RANDY BUSH

364

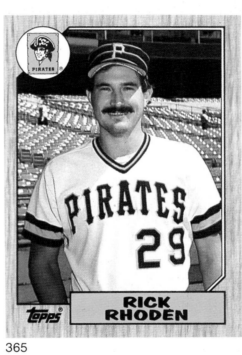

RICK RHODEN

365

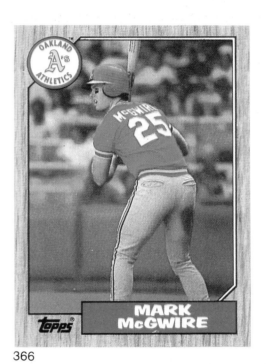

MARK McGWIRE

366

JEFF LAHTI

367

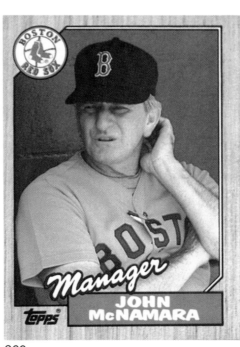

JOHN McNAMARA

368

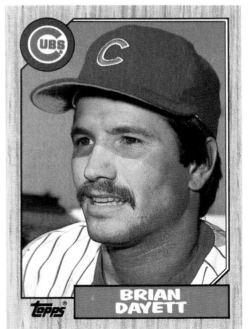

BRIAN DAYETT

369

FRED LYNN

370

MARK EICHHORN

371

JERRY MUMPHREY

372

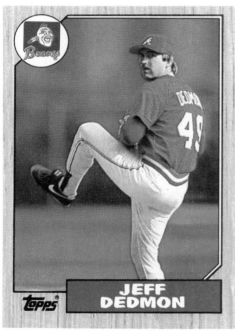

JEFF DEDMON

373

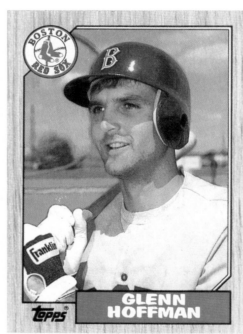

GLENN HOFFMAN

374

RON GUIDRY

375

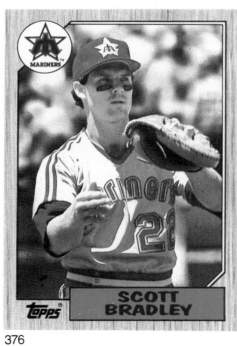

SCOTT BRADLEY

376

JOHN HENRY JOHNSON

377

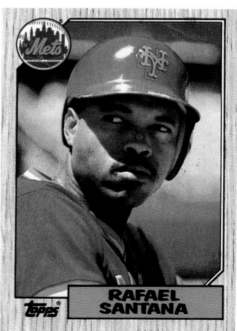

RAFAEL SANTANA

378

JOHN RUSSELL

379

RICH GOSSAGE

380

EXPOS LEADERS

381

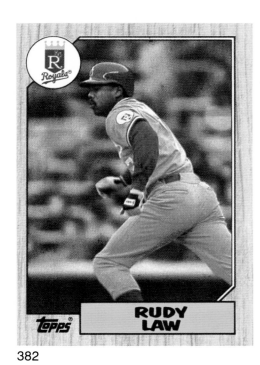

RUDY LAW

382

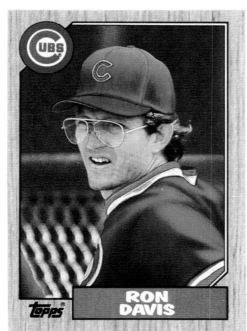

RON DAVIS

383

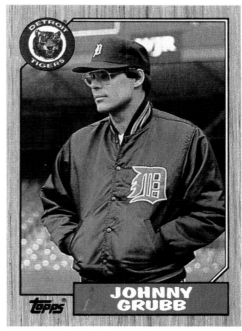

JOHNNY GRUBB

384

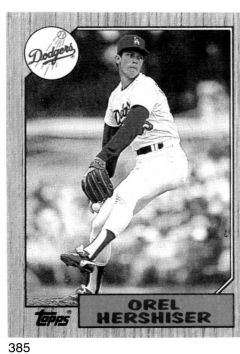

OREL HERSHISER

385

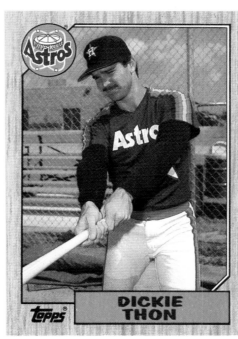

DICKIE THON

386

T.R. BRYDEN

387

GENO PETRALLI

388

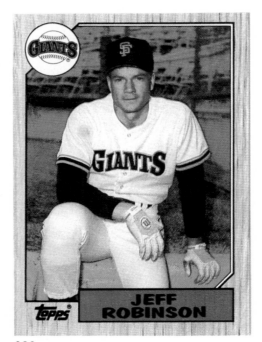

JEFF ROBINSON

389

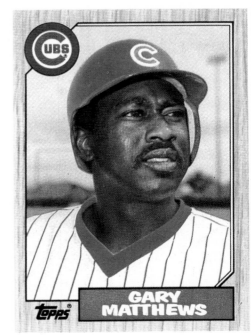

GARY MATTHEWS

390

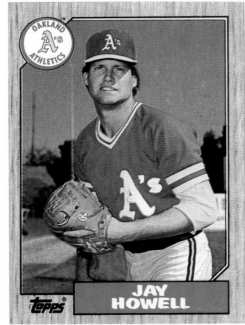

JAY HOWELL

391

265	Darrell Evans	297	Don Schulze
266	Jeff Hamilton	298	Larry Herndon
267	Howard Johnson	299	Joel Davis
268	Pat Corrales	300	Reggie Jackson
269	Cliff Speck	301	Luis Aquino
270	Jody Davis	302	Bill Schroeder
271	Mike Brown	303	Juan Berenguer
272	Andres Galarraga	304	Phil Garner
273	Gene Nelson	305	John Franco
274	Jeff Hearron	306	Red Sox Team
275	LaMarr Hoyt	307	Lee Guetterman
276	Jackie Gutierrez	308	Don Slaught
277	Juan Agosto	309	Mike Young
278	Gary Pettis	310	Frank Viola
279	Dan Plesac	311	Turn Back—1982
280	Jeffrey Leonard	312	Turn Back—1977
281	Reds Team	313	Turn Back—1972
282	Jeff Calhoun	314	Turn Back—1967
283	Doug Drabek	315	Turn Back—1962
284	John Moses	316	Brian Fisher
285	Dennis Boyd	317	Clint Hurdle
286	Mike Woodard	318	Jim Fregosi
287	Dave Von Ohlen	319	Greg Swindell
288	Tito Landrum	320	Barry Bonds
289	Bob Kipper	321	Mike Laga
290	Leon Durham	322	Chris Bando
291	Mitch Williams	323	Al Newman
292	Franklin Stubbs	324	Dave Palmer
293	Bob Rodgers	325	Garry Templeton
294	Steve Jeltz	326	Mark Gubicza
295	Len Dykstra	327	Dale Sveum
296	Andres Thomas	328	Bob Welch

1987 BASEBALL CHECKLIST CARDS 265-396

392

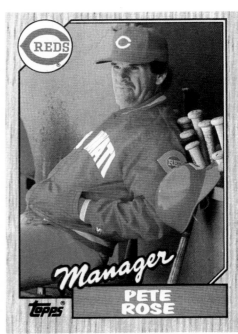

Manager
PETE ROSE

393

MIKE BIELECKI

394

DAMASO GARCIA

395

TIM LOLLAR

396

GREG WALKER

397

BRAD HAVENS

398

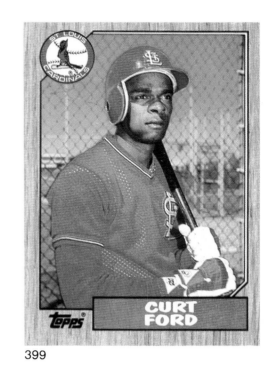

CURT FORD

399

GEORGE BRETT

400

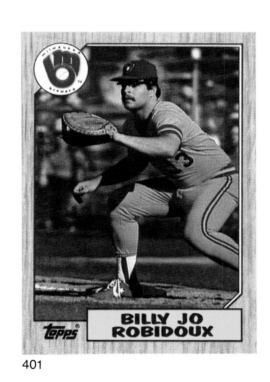

BILLY JO ROBIDOUX

401

MIKE TRUJILLO

402

JERRY ROYSTER

403

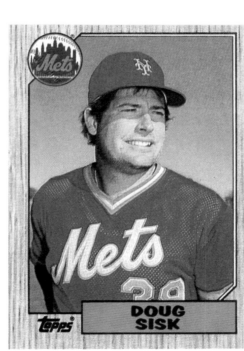

DOUG SISK

404

BROOK JACOBY

405

YANKEES LEADERS

406

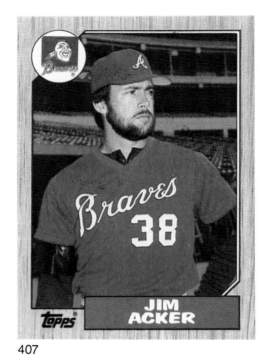

JIM ACKER

407

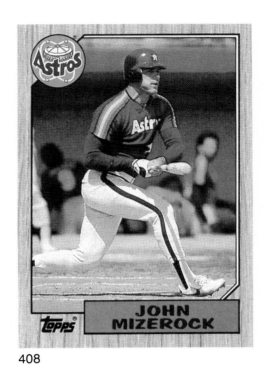

JOHN MIZEROCK

408

MILT THOMPSON

409

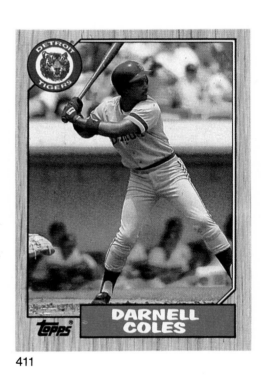

FERNANDO VALENZUELA

410

DARNELL COLES

411

ERIC DAVIS

412

MOOSE HAAS

413

JOE ORSULAK

414

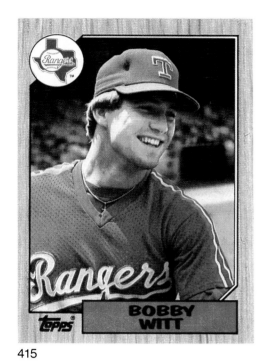

BOBBY WITT

415

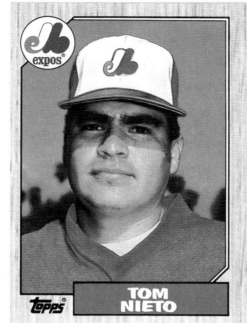

TOM NIETO

416

PAT PERRY

417

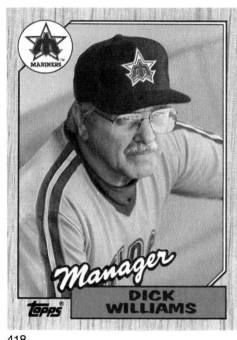

DICK WILLIAMS

418

MARK PORTUGAL

419

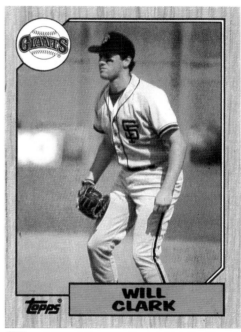

WILL CLARK

420

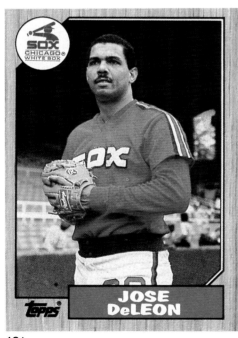

JOSE DeLEON

421

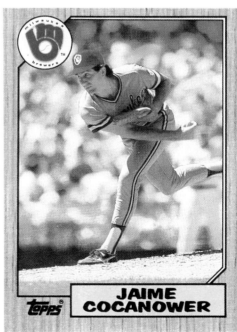

JACK HOWELL

422

JAIME COCANOWER

423

CHRIS SPEIER

424

TOM SEAVER

425

FLOYD RAYFORD

426

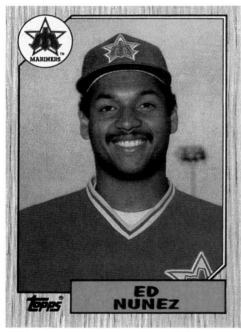
ED NUNEZ

427

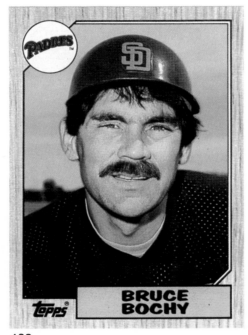
BRUCE BOCHY

428

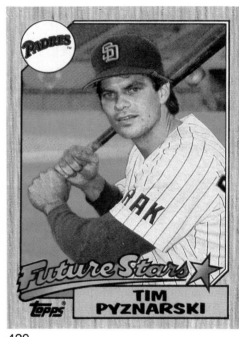
TIM PYZNARSKI

429

MIKE SCHMIDT

430

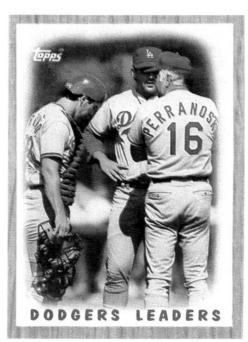
DODGERS LEADERS

431

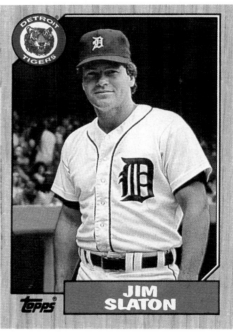
JIM SLATON

432

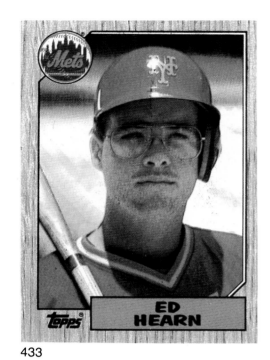

ED
HEARN

433

MIKE
FISCHLIN

434

BRUCE
SUTTER

435

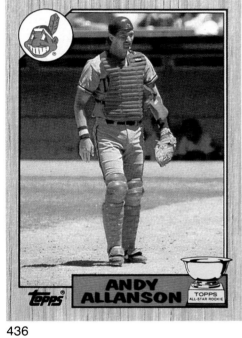

ANDY
ALLANSON

436

TED
POWER

437

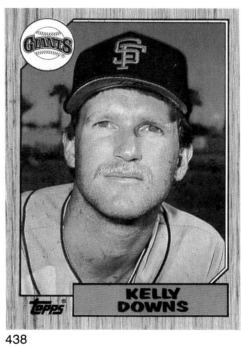

KELLY
DOWNS

438

KARL
BEST

439

WILLIE
McGEE

440

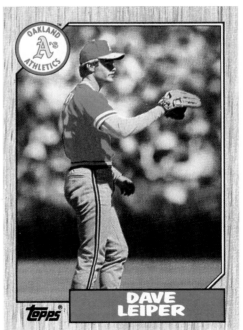

DAVE
LEIPER

441

MITCH WEBSTER

442

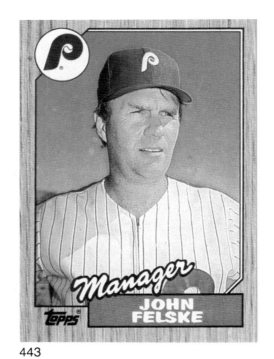

Manager
JOHN FELSKE

443

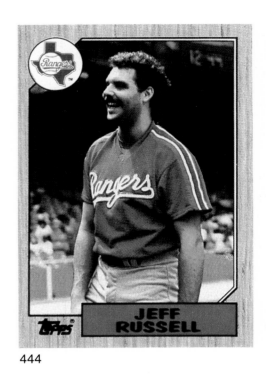

JEFF RUSSELL

444

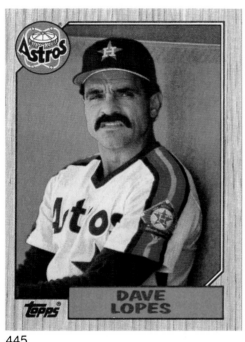

DAVE LOPES

445

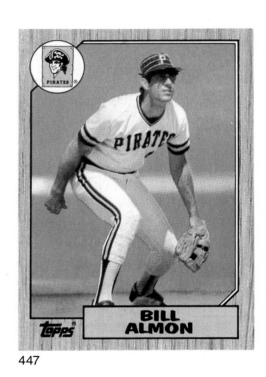

CHUCK FINLEY

446

BILL ALMON

447

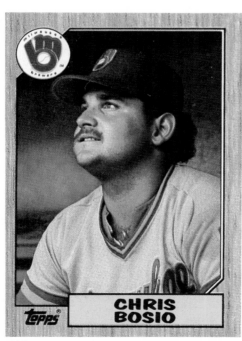

CHRIS BOSIO

448

Future Stars
PAT DODSON

449

KIRBY PUCKETT

450

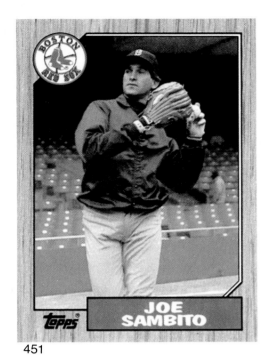

JOE
SAMBITO

451

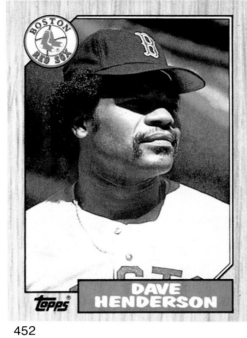

DAVE
HENDERSON

452

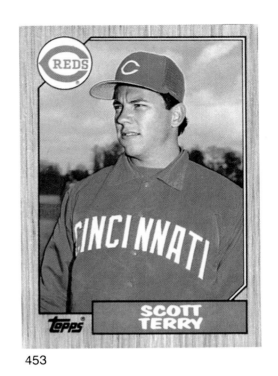

SCOTT
TERRY

453

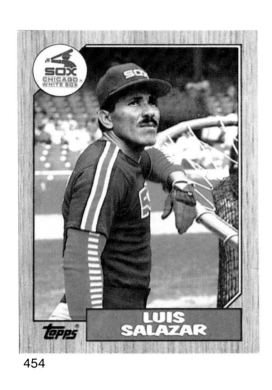

LUIS
SALAZAR

454

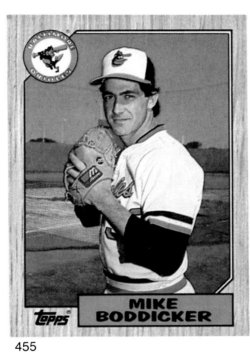

MIKE
BODDICKER

455

A's LEADERS

456

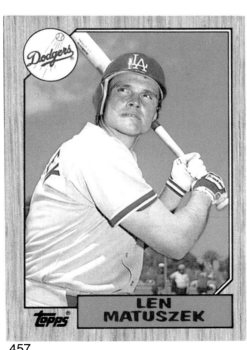

LEN
MATUSZEK

457

KELLY
GRUBER

458

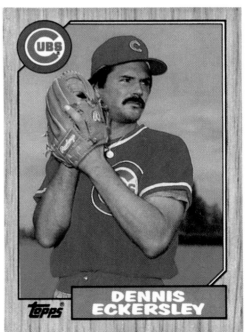

DENNIS
ECKERSLEY

459

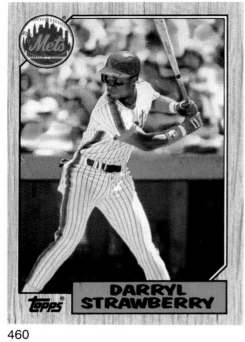

DARRYL STRAWBERRY

460

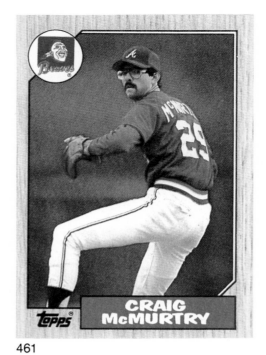

CRAIG McMURTRY

461

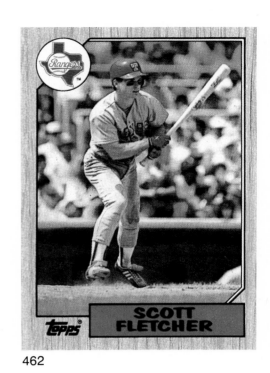

SCOTT FLETCHER

462

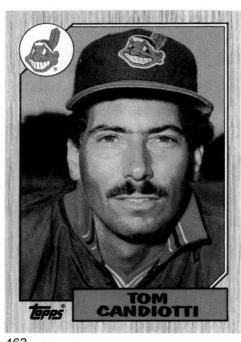

TOM CANDIOTTI

463

BUTCH WYNEGAR

464

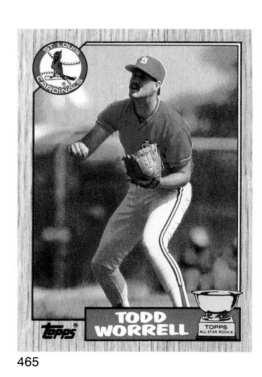

TODD WORRELL

465

KAL DANIELS

466

RANDY ST. CLAIRE

467

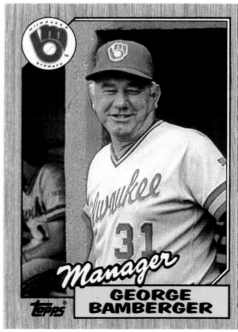

GEORGE BAMBERGER

468

MIKE DIAZ

469

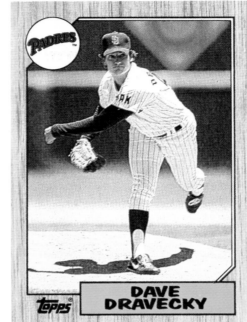

DAVE DRAVECKY

470

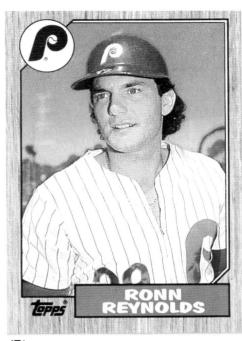

RONN REYNOLDS

471

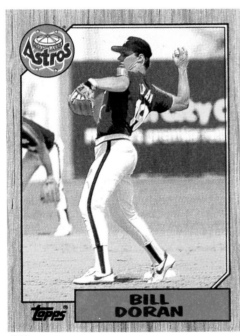

BILL DORAN

472

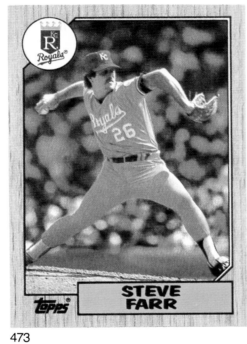

STEVE FARR

473

JERRY NARRON

474

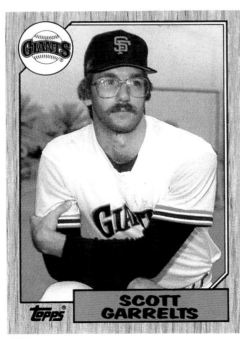

SCOTT GARRELTS

475

DANNY TARTABULL

476

KEN HOWELL

477

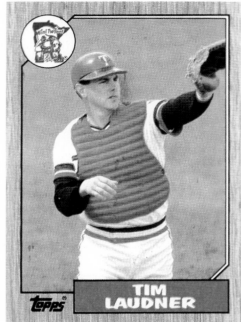

TIM
LAUDNER

478

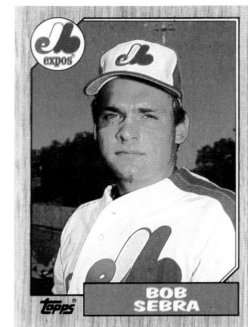

BOB
SEBRA

479

JIM RICE

480

PHILLIES LEADERS

481

DARYL
BOSTON

482

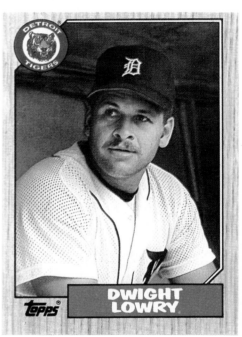

DWIGHT
LOWRY

483

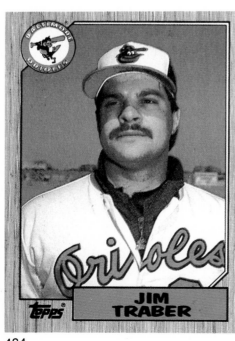

JIM
TRABER

484

TONY
FERNANDEZ

485

OTIS
NIXON

486

DAVE GUMPERT

487

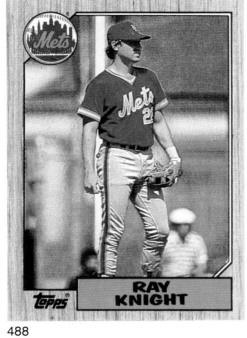

RAY KNIGHT

488

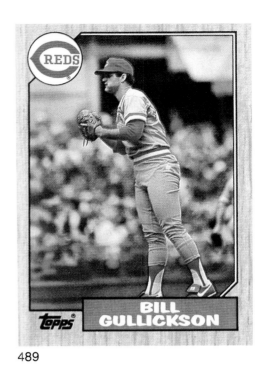

BILL GULLICKSON

489

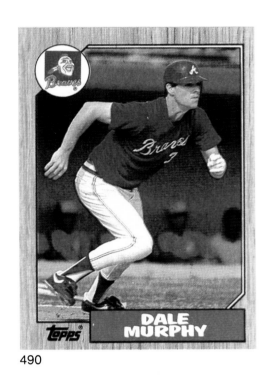

DALE MURPHY

490

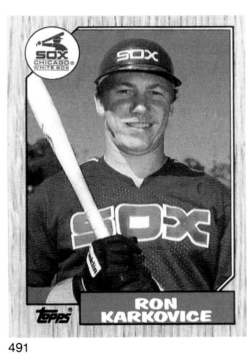

RON KARKOVICE

491

MIKE HEATH

492

TOM LASORDA

493

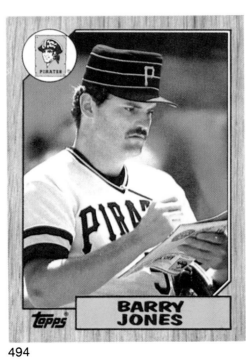

BARRY JONES

494

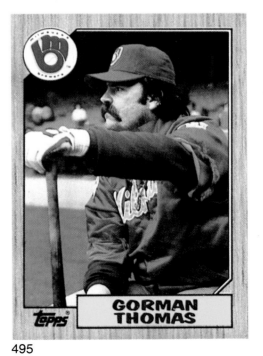

GORMAN THOMAS

495

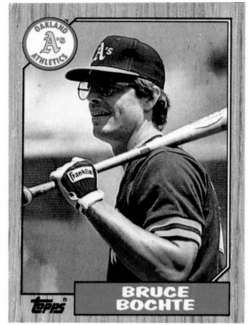

496

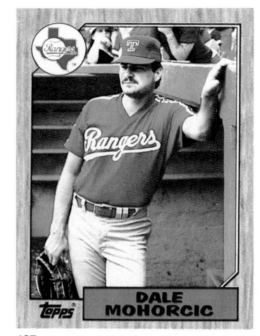

497

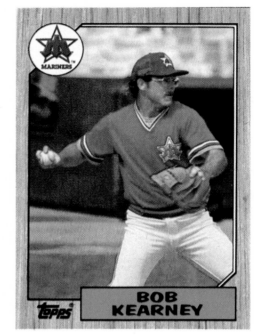

498

499

500

501

502

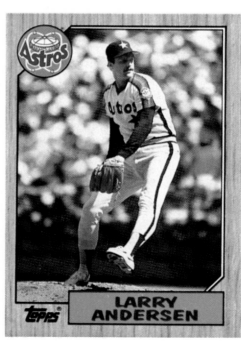

503

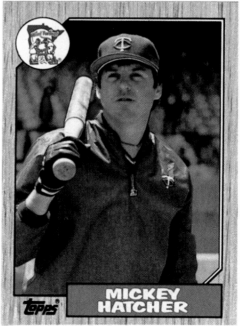

504

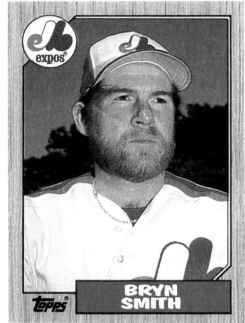

BRYN SMITH

505

ORIOLES LEADERS

506

DAVE STAPLETON

507

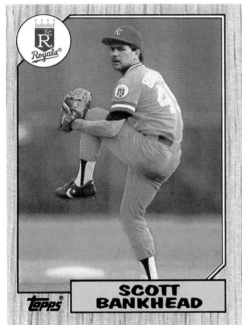

SCOTT BANKHEAD

508

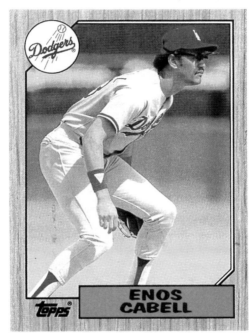

ENOS CABELL

509

TOM HENKE

510

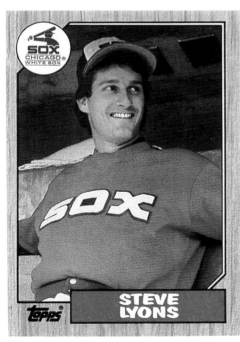

STEVE LYONS

511

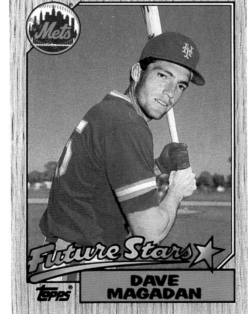

DAVE MAGADAN

512

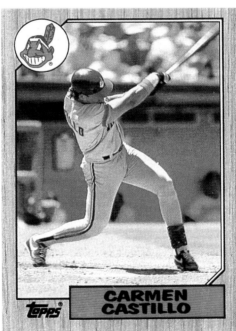

CARMEN CASTILLO

513

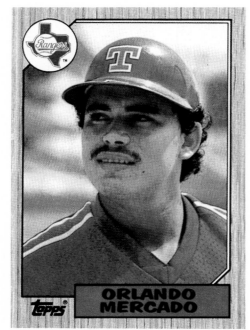

ORLANDO MERCADO

514

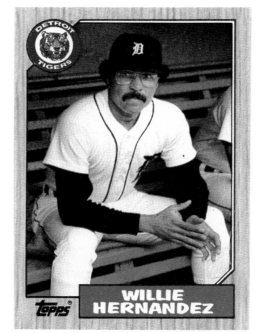

WILLIE HERNANDEZ

515

TED SIMMONS

516

MARIO SOTO

517

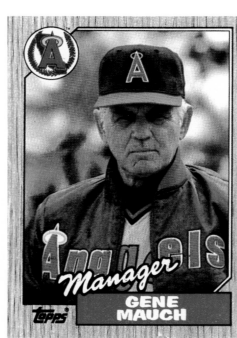

GENE MAUCH

518

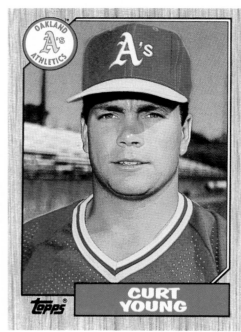

CURT YOUNG

519

JACK CLARK

520

RICK REUSCHEL

521

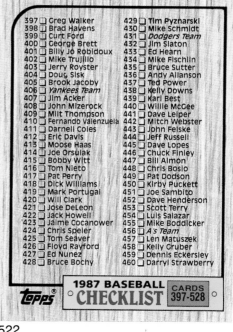

397	Greg Walker	429	Tim Pyznarski
398	Brad Havens	430	Mike Schmidt
399	Curt Ford	431	Dodgers Team
400	George Brett	432	Jim Slaton
401	Billy Jo Robidoux	433	Ed Hearn
402	Mike Trujillo	434	Mike Fischlin
403	Jerry Royster	435	Bruce Sutter
404	Doug Sisk	436	Andy Allanson
405	Brook Jacoby	437	Ted Power
406	Yankees Team	438	Kelly Downs
407	Jim Acker	439	Karl Best
408	John Mizerock	440	Willie McGee
409	Milt Thompson	441	Dave Leiper
410	Fernando Valenzuela	442	Mitch Webster
411	Darnell Coles	443	John Felske
412	Eric Davis	444	Jeff Russell
413	Moose Haas	445	Dave Lopes
414	Joe Orsulak	446	Chuck Finley
415	Bobby Witt	447	Bill Almon
416	Tom Nieto	448	Chris Bosio
417	Pat Perry	449	Pat Dodson
418	Dick Williams	450	Kirby Puckett
419	Mark Portugal	451	Joe Sambito
420	Will Clark	452	Dave Henderson
421	Jose DeLeon	453	Scott Terry
422	Jack Howell	454	Luis Salazar
423	Jaime Cocanower	455	Mike Boddicker
424	Chris Speier	456	A's Team
425	Tom Seaver	457	Len Matuszek
426	Floyd Rayford	458	Kelly Gruber
427	Ed Nunez	459	Dennis Eckersley
428	Bruce Bochy	460	Darryl Strawberry

1987 BASEBALL CHECKLIST CARDS 397-528

522

EARNIE
RILES

523

BOB
SHIRLEY

524

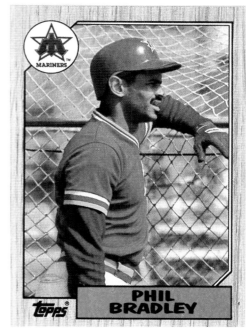

PHIL
BRADLEY

525

ROGER
MASON

526

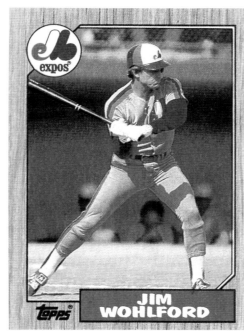

JIM
WOHLFORD

527

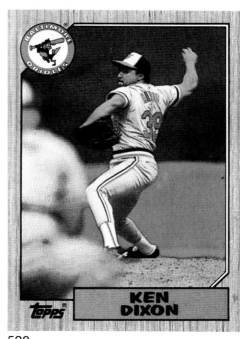

KEN
DIXON

528

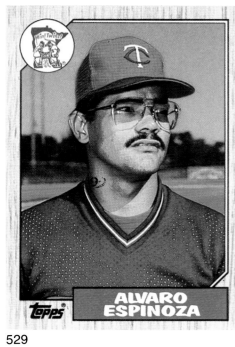

ALVARO
ESPINOZA

529

TONY
GWYNN

530

ASTROS LEADERS

531

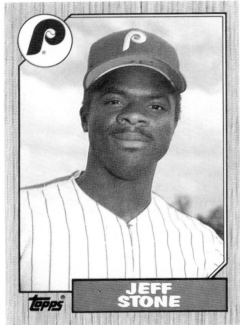

JEFF STONE

532

ARGENIS SALAZAR

533

SCOTT SANDERSON

534

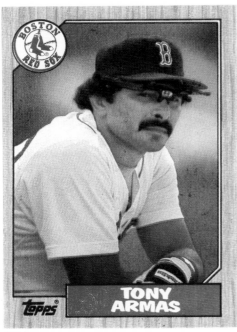

TONY ARMAS

535

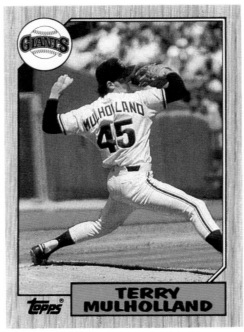

TERRY MULHOLLAND

536

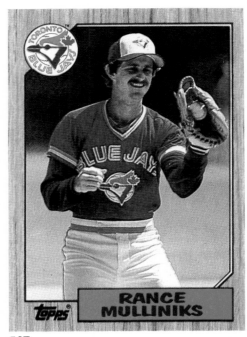

RANCE MULLINIKS

537

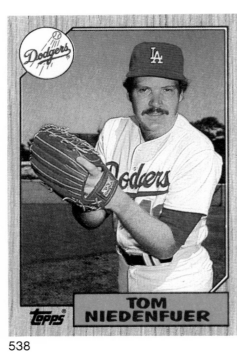

TOM NIEDENFUER

538

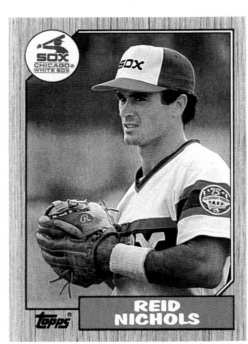

REID NICHOLS

539

TERRY KENNEDY

540

RAFAEL
BELLIARD

541

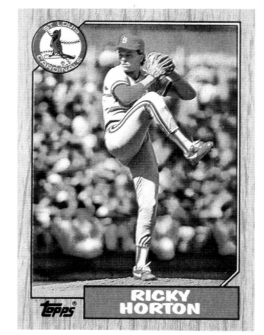

RICKY
HORTON

542

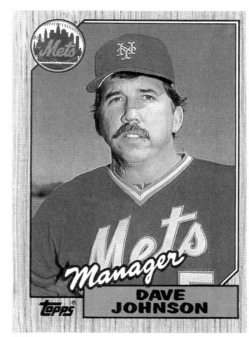

DAVE
JOHNSON

543

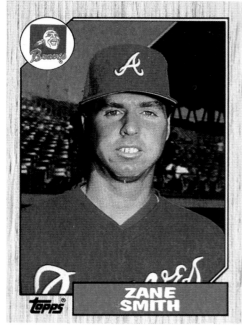

ZANE
SMITH

544

BUDDY
BELL

545

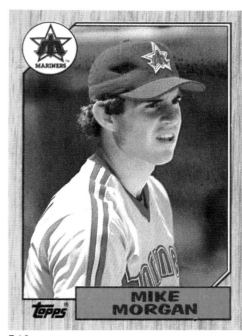

MIKE
MORGAN

546

ROB
DEER

547

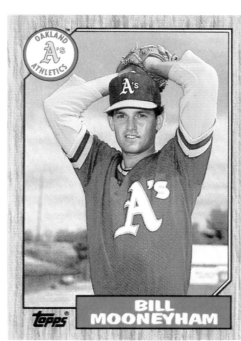

BILL
MOONEYHAM

548

BOB
MELVIN

549

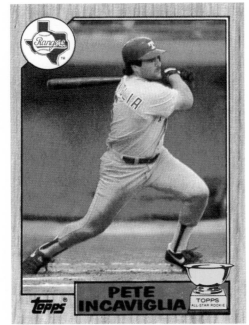

PETE INCAVIGLIA

550

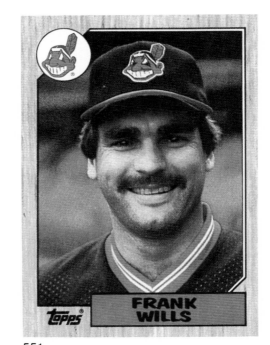

FRANK WILLS

551

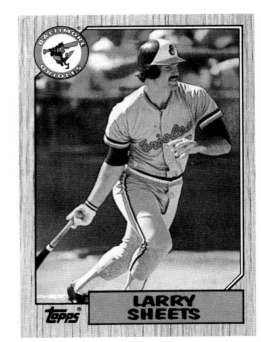

LARRY SHEETS

552

MIKE MADDUX

553

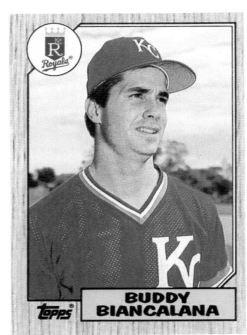

BUDDY BIANCALANA

554

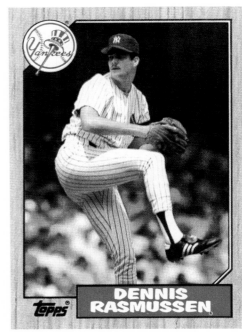

DENNIS RASMUSSEN

555

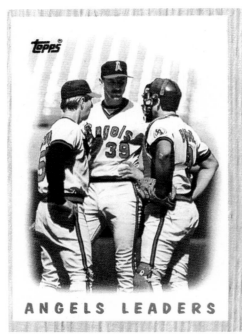

ANGELS LEADERS

556

JOHN CERUTTI

557

GREG GAGNE

558

LANCE McCULLERS

559

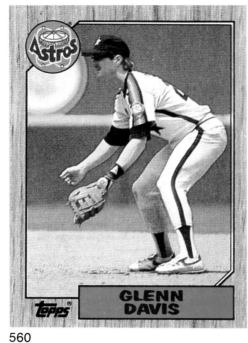

GLENN DAVIS

560

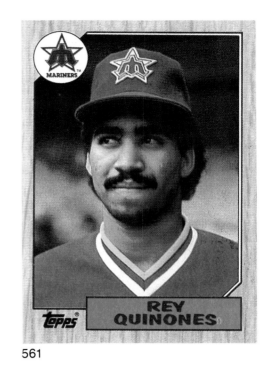

REY QUINONES

561

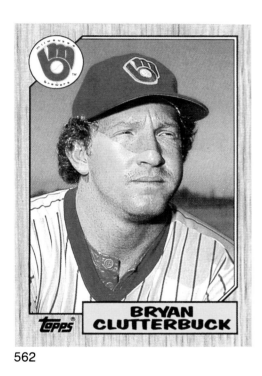

BRYAN CLUTTERBUCK

562

JOHN STEFERO

563

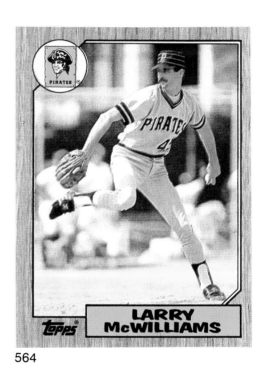

LARRY McWILLIAMS

564

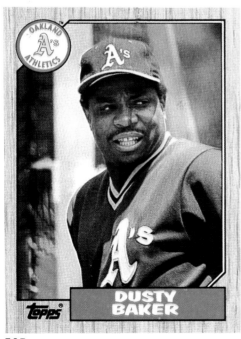

DUSTY BAKER

565

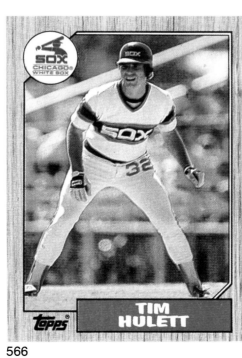

TIM HULETT

566

GREG MATHEWS

567

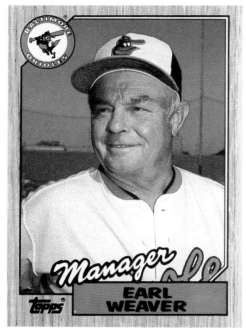

EARL WEAVER

568

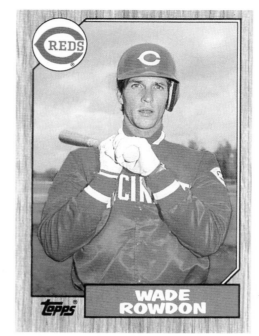

WADE ROWDON

569

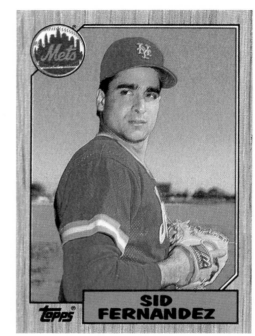

SID FERNANDEZ

570

OZZIE VIRGIL

571

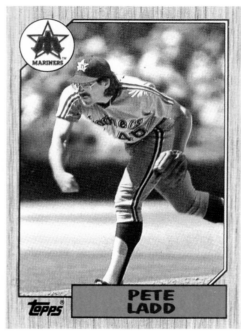

PETE LADD

572

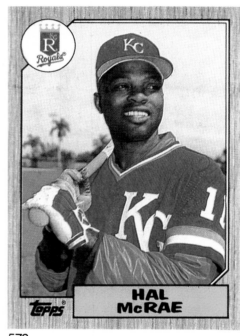

HAL McRAE

573

MANNY LEE

574

PAT TABLER

575

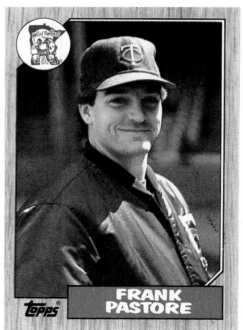

FRANK PASTORE

576

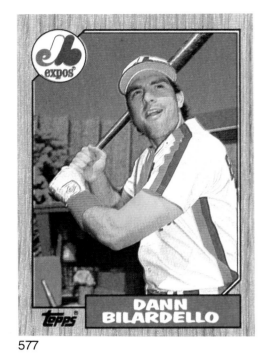

DANN BILARDELLO

577

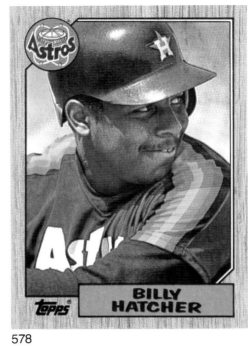

BILLY HATCHER

578

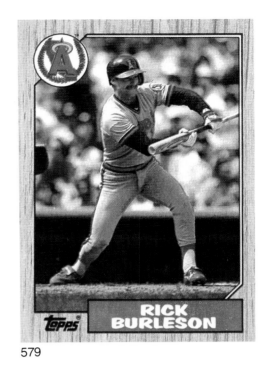

RICK BURLESON

579

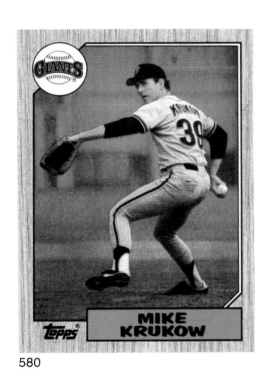

MIKE KRUKOW

580

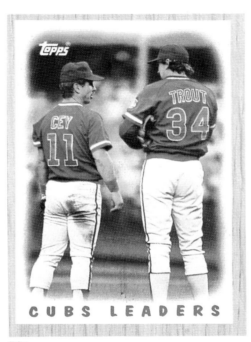

CUBS LEADERS

581

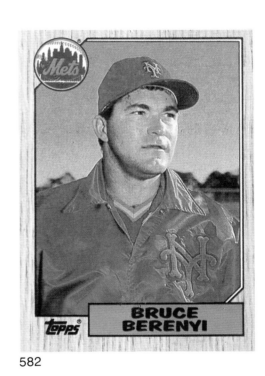

BRUCE BERENYI

582

JUNIOR ORTIZ

583

RON KITTLE

584

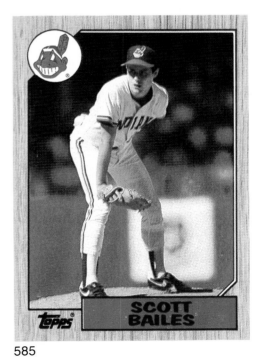

SCOTT BAILES

585

BEN OGLIVIE

586

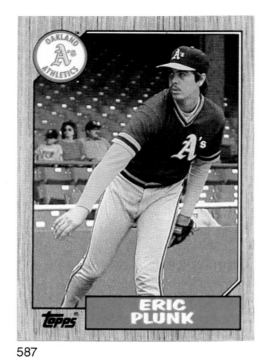

ERIC PLUNK

587

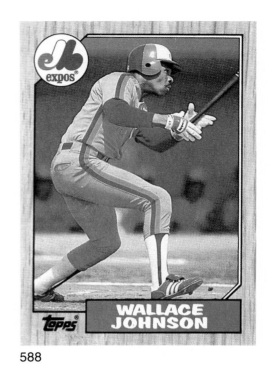

WALLACE JOHNSON

588

STEVE CRAWFORD

589

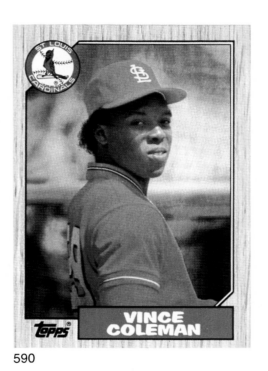

VINCE COLEMAN

590

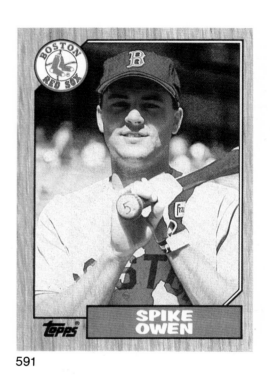

SPIKE OWEN

591

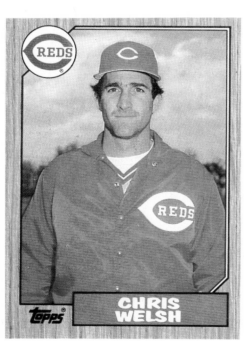

CHRIS WELSH

592

Manager

CHUCK TANNER

593

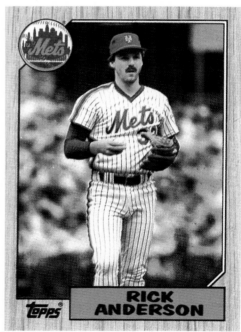

RICK ANDERSON

594

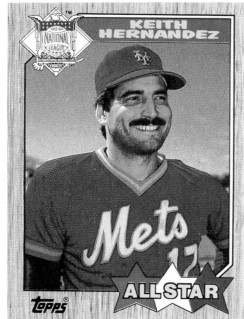

595

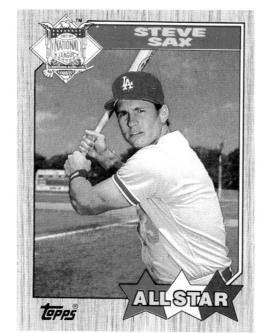

596

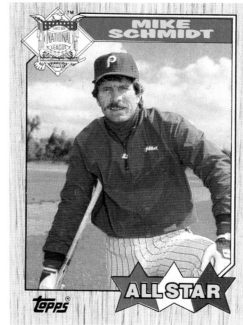

597

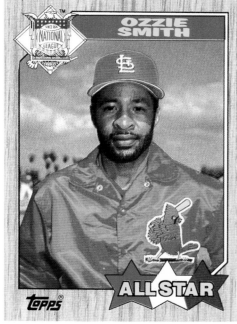

598

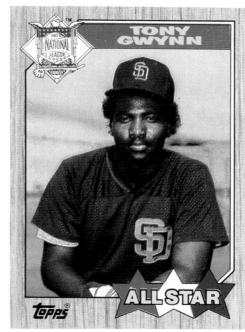

599

600

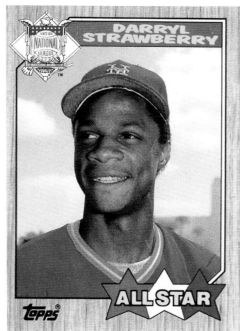

601

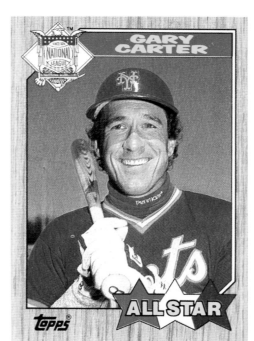

602

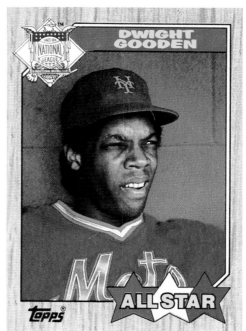

603

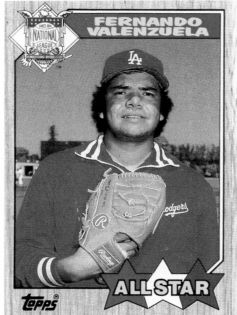
604

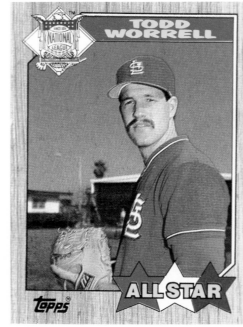
605

606

607

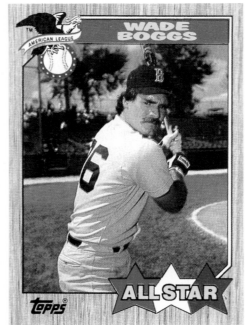
608

609

610

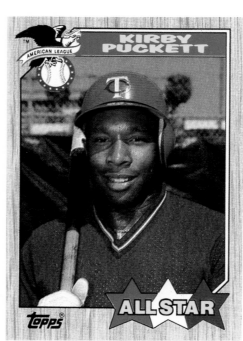
611

612

613

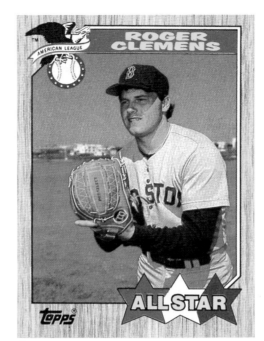

614

615

616

617

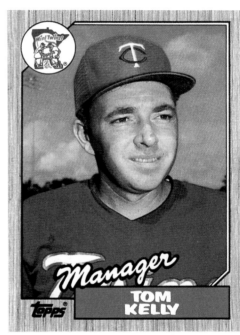

618

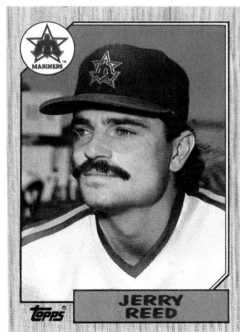

619

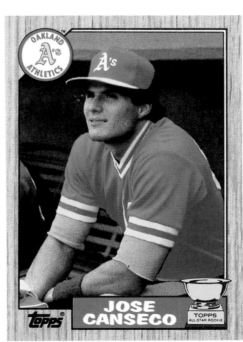

620

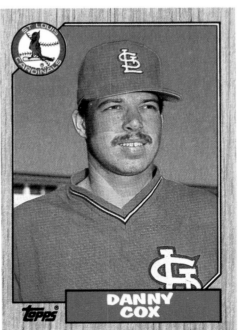

621

GLENN BRAGGS

622

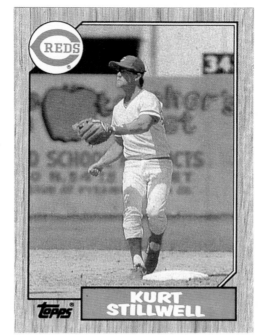

KURT STILLWELL

623

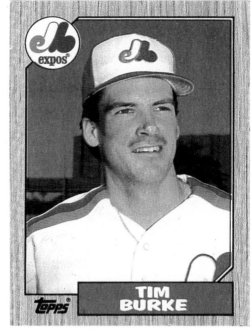

TIM BURKE

624

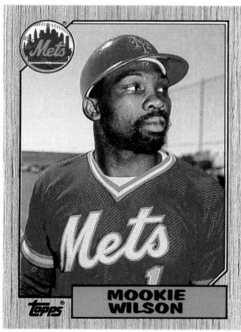

MOOKIE WILSON

625

JOEL SKINNER

626

KEN OBERKFELL

627

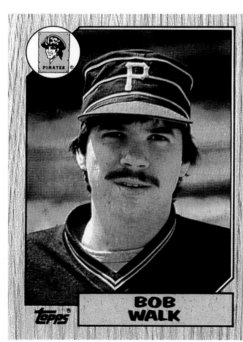

BOB WALK

628

LARRY PARRISH

629

JOHN CANDELARIA

630

TIGERS LEADERS

631

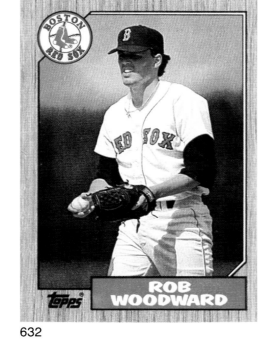

ROB WOODWARD

632

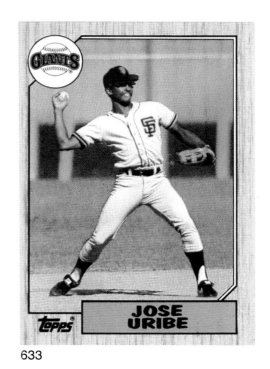

JOSE URIBE

633

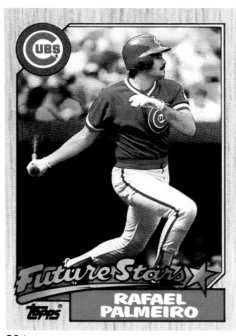

RAFAEL PALMEIRO

634

KEN SCHROM

635

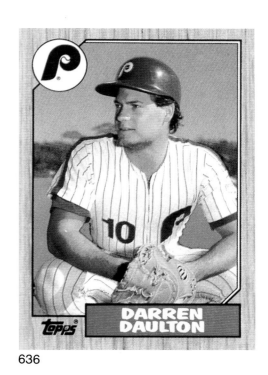

DARREN DAULTON

636

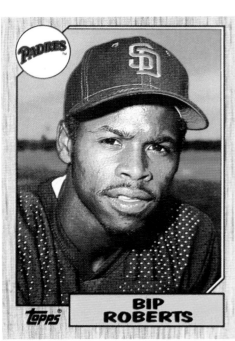

BIP ROBERTS

637

RICH BORDI

638

GERALD PERRY

639

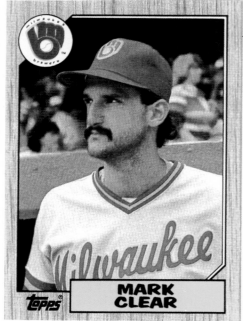

MARK CLEAR

640

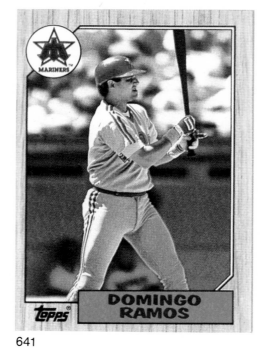

DOMINGO RAMOS

641

AL PULIDO

642

RON SHEPHERD

643

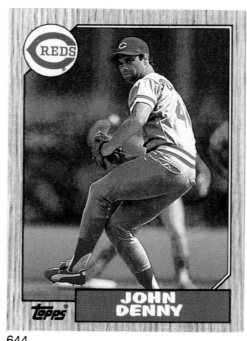

JOHN DENNY

644

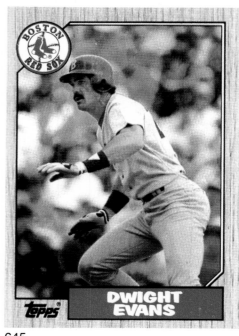

DWIGHT EVANS

645

MIKE MASON

646

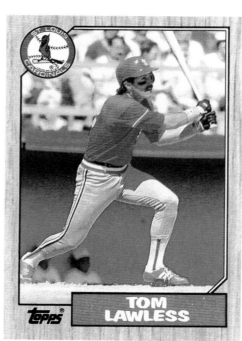

TOM LAWLESS

647

BARRY LARKIN

648

MICKEY
TETTLETON

649

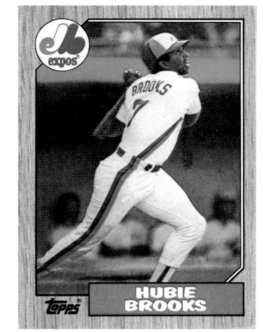

HUBIE
BROOKS

650

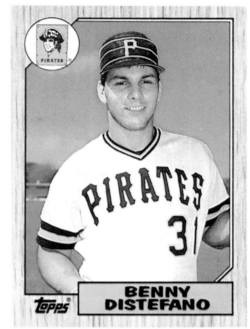

BENNY
DISTEFANO

651

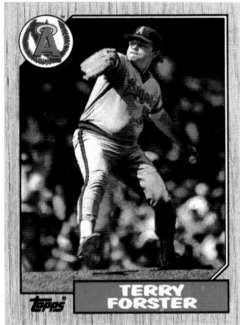

TERRY FORSTER

652

KEVIN
MITCHELL

653

529	Alvaro Espinoza	561	Rey Quinones
530	Tony Gwynn	562	Bryan Clutterbuck
531	Astros Team	563	John Stefero
532	Jeff Stone	564	Larry McWilliams
533	Argenis Salazar	565	Dusty Baker
534	Scott Sanderson	566	Tim Hulett
535	Tony Armas	567	Greg Mathews
536	Terry Mulholland	568	Earl Weaver
537	Rance Mulliniks	569	Wade Rowdon
538	Tom Niedenfuer	570	Sid Fernandez
539	Reid Nichols	571	Ozzie Virgil
540	Terry Kennedy	572	Pete Ladd
541	Rafael Belliard	573	Hal McRae
542	Ricky Horton	574	Manny Lee
543	Dave Johnson	575	Pat Tabler
544	Zane Smith	576	Frank Pastore
545	Buddy Bell	577	Dann Bilardello
546	Mike Morgan	578	Billy Hatcher
547	Rob Deer	579	Rick Burleson
548	Bill Mooneyham	580	Mike Krukow
549	Bob Melvin	581	Cubs Team
550	Pete Incaviglia	582	Bruce Berenyi
551	Frank Wills	583	Junior Ortiz
552	Larry Sheets	584	Ron Kittle
553	Mike Maddux	585	Scott Bailes
554	Buddy Biancalana	586	Ben Oglivie
555	Dennis Rasmussen	587	Eric Plunk
556	Angels Team	588	Wallace Johnson
557	John Cerutti	589	Steve Crawford
558	Greg Gagne	590	Vince Coleman
559	Lance McCullers	591	Spike Owen
560	Glenn Davis	592	Chris Welsh

1987 BASEBALL CHECKLIST
CARDS 529-660

654

JESSE
BARFIELD

655

RANGERS LEADERS

656

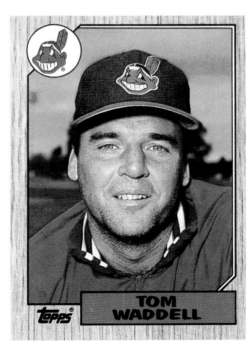

TOM
WADDELL

657

ROBBY THOMPSON

658

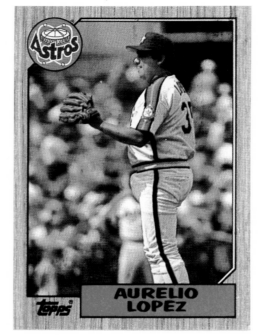

AURELIO LOPEZ

659

BOB HORNER

660

LOU WHITAKER

661

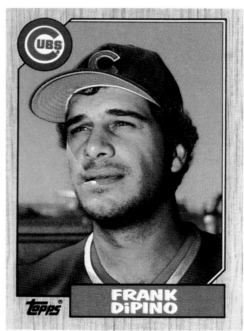

FRANK DiPINO

662

CLIFF JOHNSON

663

MIKE MARSHALL

664

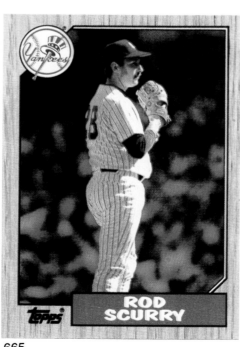

ROD SCURRY

665

VON HAYES

666

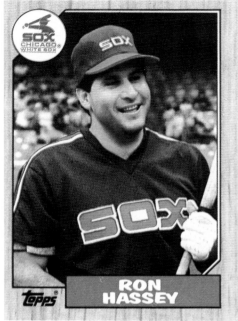

RON
HASSEY

667

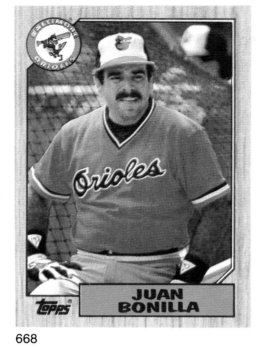

JUAN
BONILLA

668

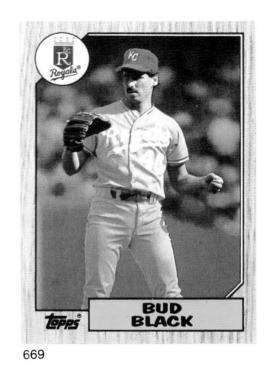

BUD
BLACK

669

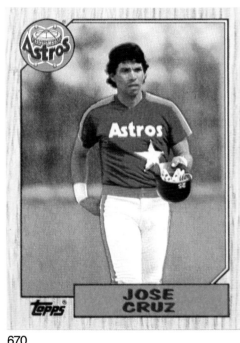

JOSE
CRUZ

670

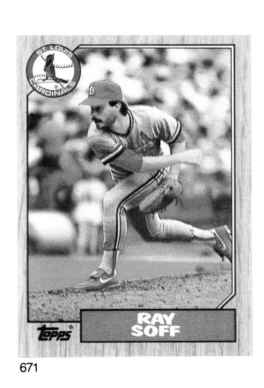

RAY SOFF

671

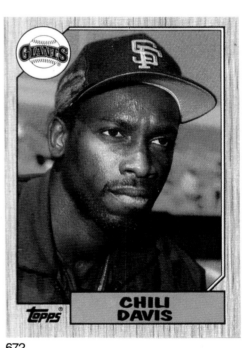

CHILI
DAVIS

672

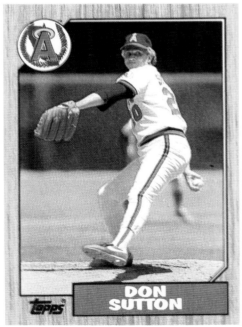

DON
SUTTON

673

BILL
CAMPBELL

674

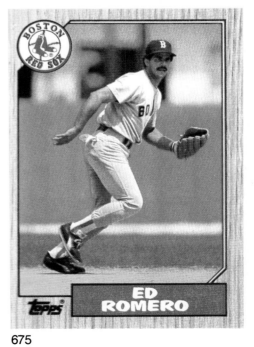

ED
ROMERO

675

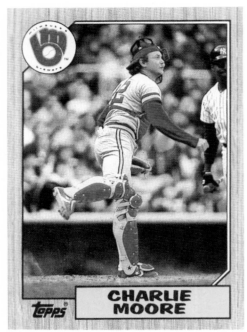

CHARLIE MOORE

676

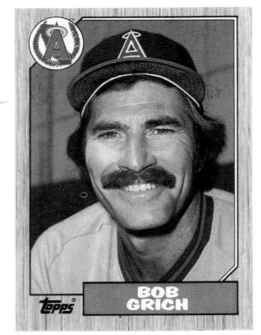

BOB GRICH

677

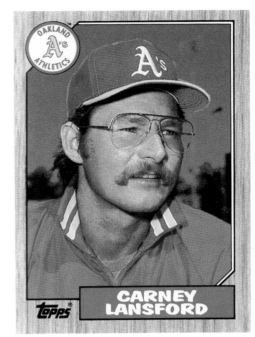

CARNEY LANSFORD

678

KENT HRBEK

679

RYNE SANDBERG

680

GEORGE BELL

681

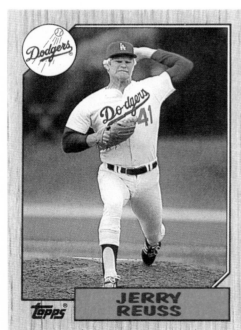

JERRY REUSS

682

GARY ROENICKE

683

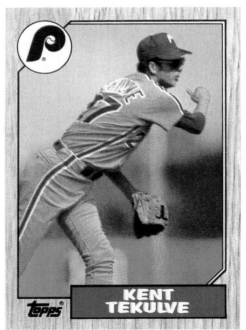

KENT TEKULVE

684

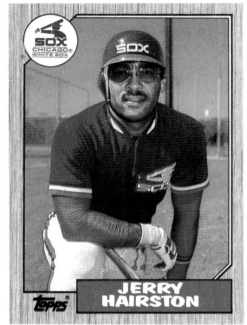

JERRY
HAIRSTON

685

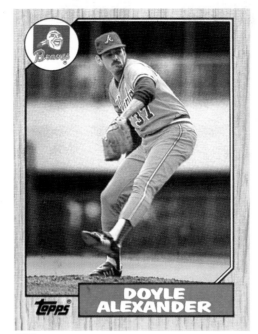

DOYLE
ALEXANDER

686

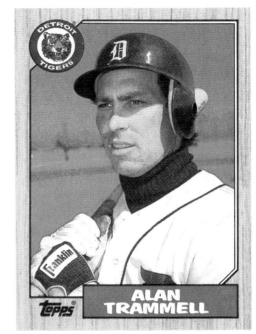

ALAN
TRAMMELL

687

JUAN
BENIQUEZ

688

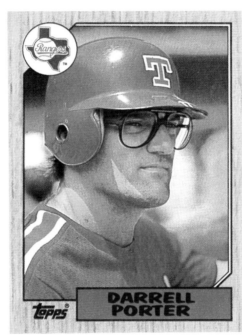

DARRELL
PORTER

689

DANE
IORG

690

DAVE
PARKER

691

FRANK
WHITE

692

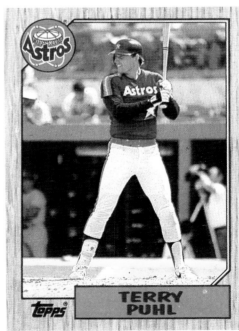

TERRY
PUHL

693

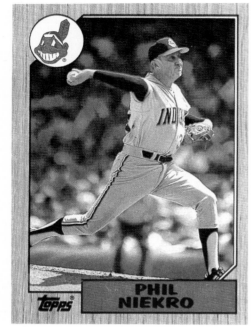

PHIL
NIEKRO

694

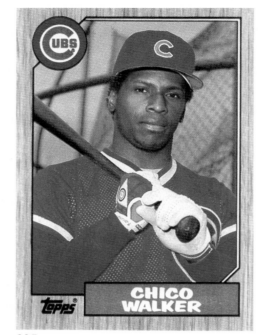

CHICO
WALKER

695

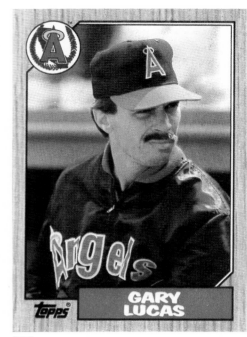

GARY
LUCAS

696

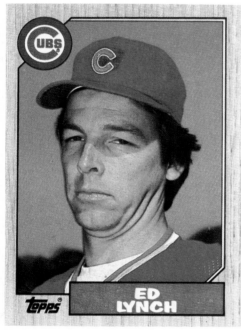

ED
LYNCH

697

ERNIE
WHITT

698

KEN
LANDREAUX

699

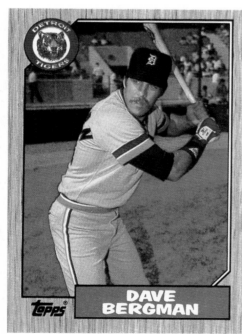

DAVE
BERGMAN

700

WILLIE
RANDOLPH

701

GREG
GROSS

702

DAVE
SCHMIDT

703

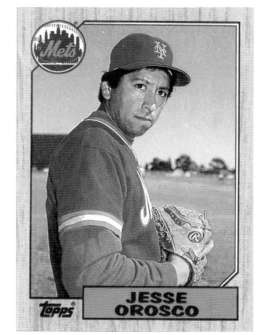

JESSE
OROSCO

704

BRUCE
HURST

705

RICK
MANNING

706

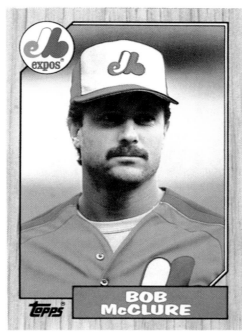

BOB
McCLURE

707

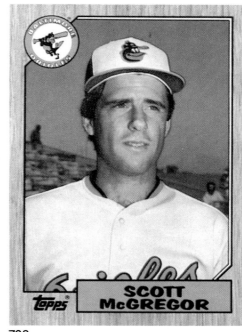

SCOTT
McGREGOR

708

DAVE
KINGMAN

709

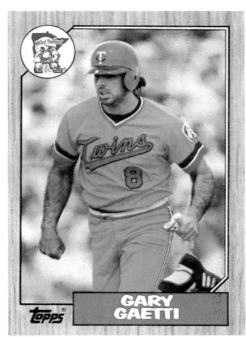

GARY
GAETTI

710

KEN
GRIFFEY

711

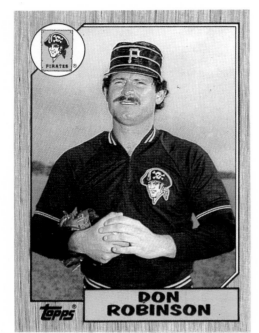

DON
ROBINSON

712

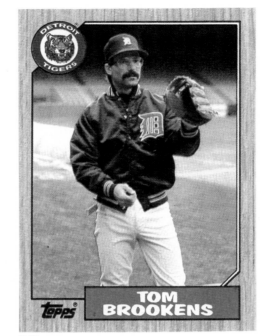

TOM
BROOKENS

713

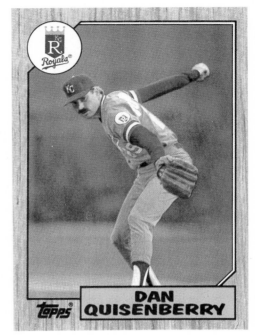

DAN
QUISENBERRY

714

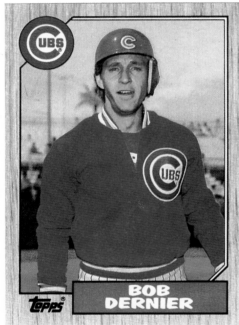

BOB
DERNIER

715

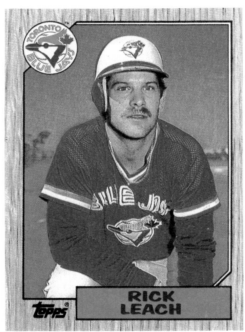

RICK
LEACH

716

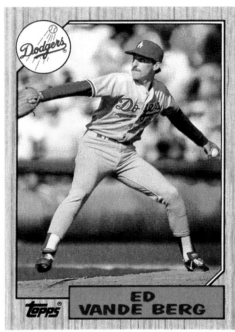

ED
VANDE BERG

717

STEVE
CARLTON

718

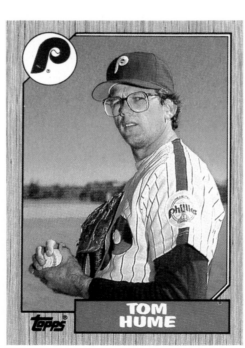

TOM HUME

719

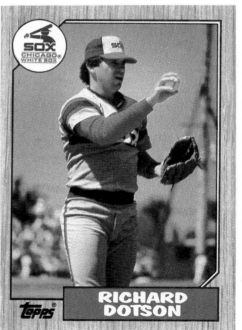

RICHARD
DOTSON

720

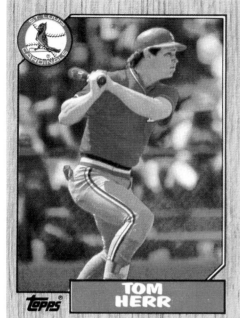

TOM HERR

721

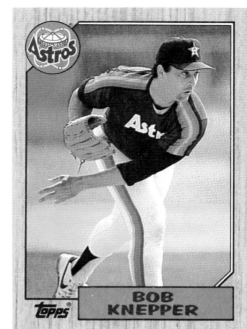

BOB KNEPPER

722

BRETT BUTLER

723

GREG MINTON

724

GEORGE HENDRICK

725

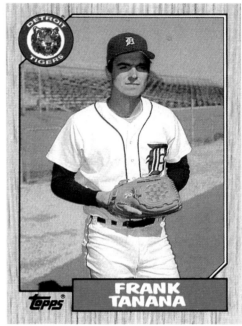

FRANK TANANA

726

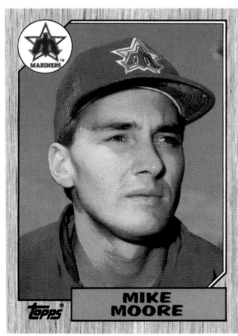

MIKE MOORE

727

TIPPY MARTINEZ

728

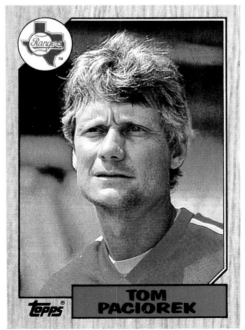

TOM PACIOREK

729

ERIC SHOW

730

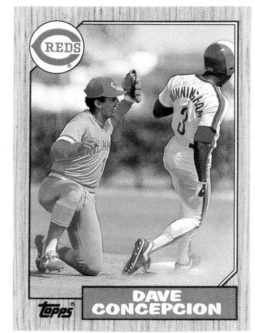

DAVE CONCEPCION

731

MANNY TRILLO

732

BILL CAUDILL

733

BILL MADLOCK

734

RICKEY HENDERSON

735

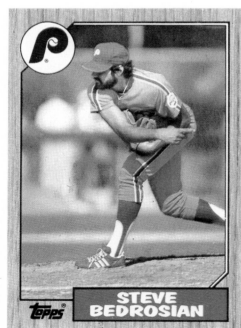

STEVE BEDROSIAN

736

FLOYD BANNISTER

737

JORGE ORTA

738

CHET LEMON

739

RICH GEDMAN

740

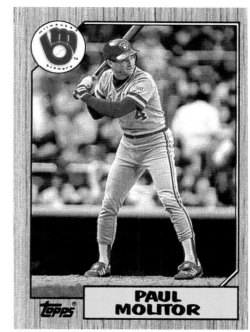

PAUL MOLITOR

741

ANDY McGAFFIGAN

742

DWAYNE MURPHY

743

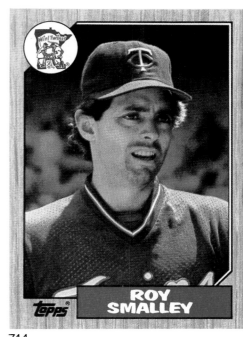

ROY SMALLEY

744

GLENN HUBBARD

745

BOB OJEDA

746

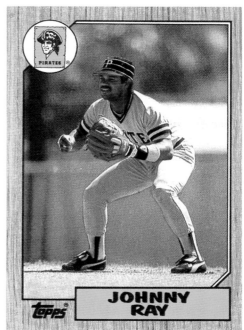

JOHNNY RAY

747

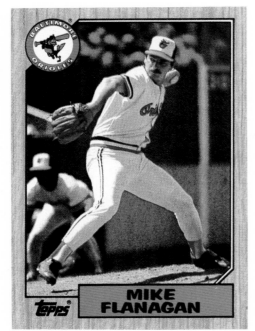

MIKE
FLANAGAN

748

OZZIE
SMITH

749

STEVE
TROUT

750

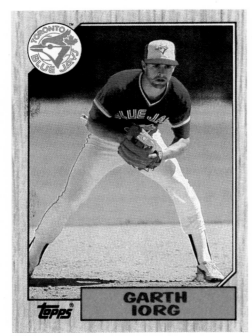

GARTH
IORG

751

DAN
PETRY

752

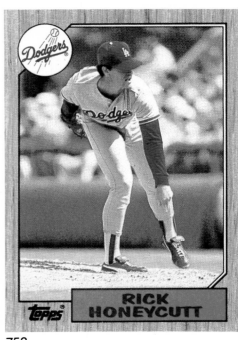

RICK
HONEYCUTT

753

DAVE
LaPOINT

754

LUIS
AGUAYO

755

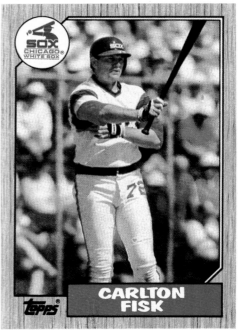

CARLTON
FISK

756

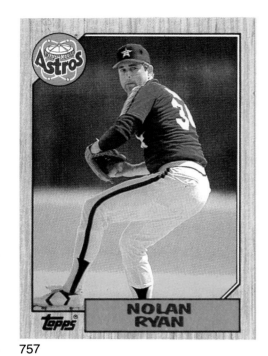

NOLAN RYAN

757

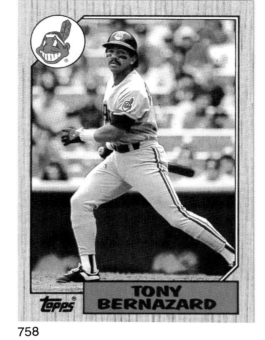

TONY BERNAZARD

758

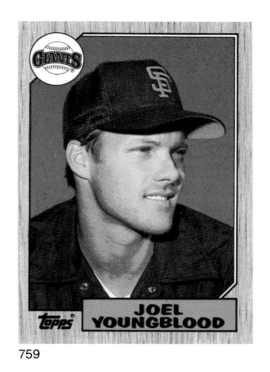

JOEL YOUNGBLOOD

759

MIKE WITT

760

GREG PRYOR

761

GARY WARD

762

TIM FLANNERY

763

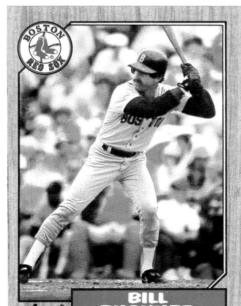

BILL BUCKNER

764

KIRK GIBSON

765

DON AASE

766

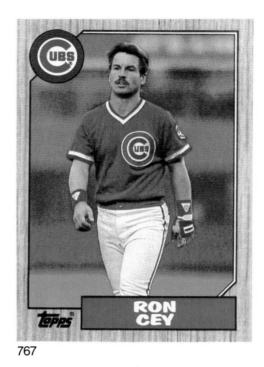

RON CEY

767

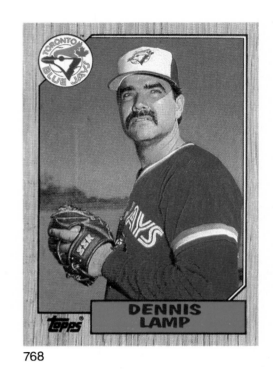

DENNIS LAMP

768

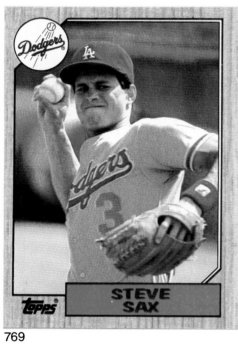

STEVE SAX

769

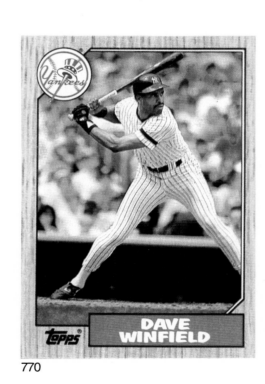

DAVE WINFIELD

770

SHANE RAWLEY

771

HAROLD BAINES

772

ROBIN YOUNT

773

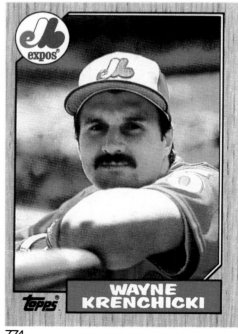

WAYNE KRENCHICKI

774

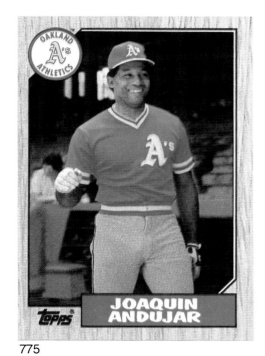
JOAQUIN ANDUJAR

775

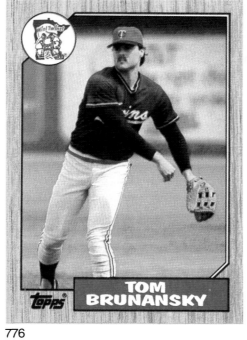
TOM BRUNANSKY

776

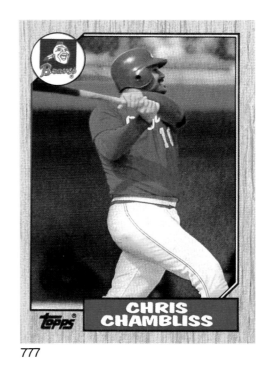
CHRIS CHAMBLISS

777

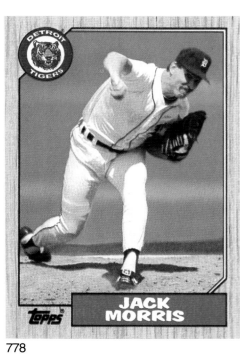
JACK MORRIS

778

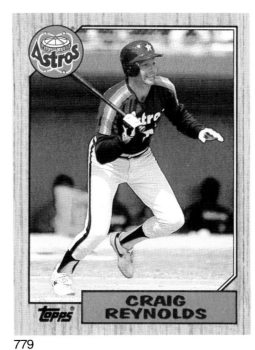
CRAIG REYNOLDS

779

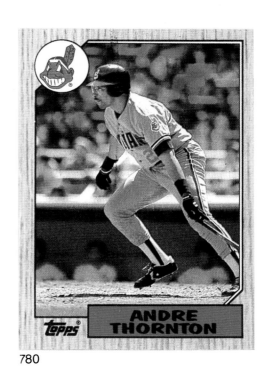
ANDRE THORNTON

780

ATLEE HAMMAKER

781

BRIAN DOWNING

782

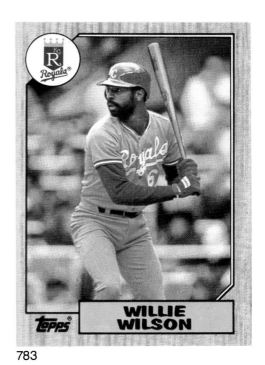
WILLIE WILSON

783

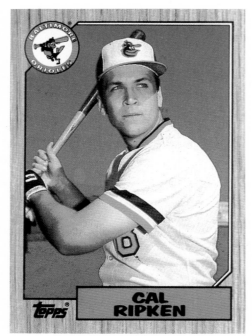

CAL
RIPKEN

784

TERRY
FRANCONA

785

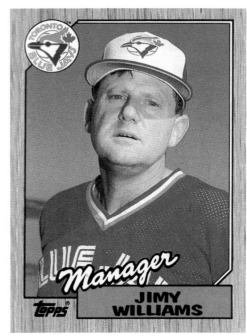

Manager

JIMY
WILLIAMS

786

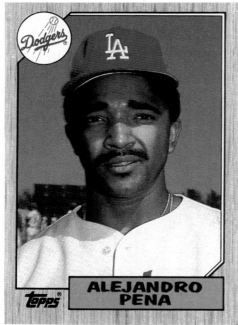

ALEJANDRO
PENA

787

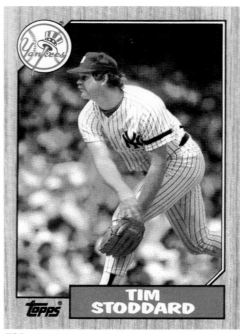

TIM
STODDARD

788

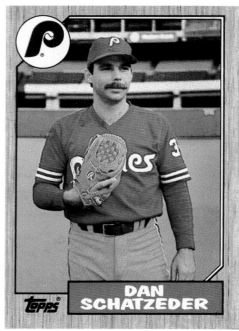

DAN
SCHATZEDER

789

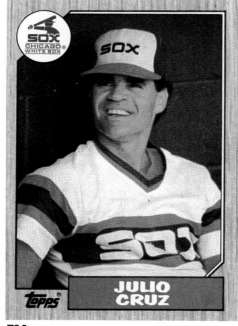

JULIO
CRUZ

790

LANCE
PARRISH

791

661	Lou Whitaker	693	Terry Puhl
662	Frank DiPino	694	Phil Niekro
663	Cliff Johnson	695	Chico Walker
664	Mike Marshall	696	Gary Lucas
665	Rod Scurry	697	Ed Lynch
666	Von Hayes	698	Ernie Whitt
667	Ron Hassey	699	Ken Landreaux
668	Juan Bonilla	700	Dave Bergman
669	Bud Black	701	Willie Randolph
670	Jose Cruz	702	Greg Gross
671	Ray Soff	703	Dave Schmidt
672	Chili Davis	704	Jesse Orosco
673	Don Sutton	705	Bruce Hurst
674	Bill Campbell	706	Rick Manning
675	Ed Romero	707	Bob McClure
676	Charlie Moore	708	Scott McGregor
677	Carney Lansford	709	Dave Kingman
678	Carney Lansford	710	Gary Gaetti
679	Kent Hrbek	711	Ken Griffey
680	Ryne Sandberg	712	Don Robinson
681	George Bell	713	Tom Brookens
682	Jerry Reuss	714	Dan Quisenberry
683	Gary Roenicke	715	Bob Dernier
684	Kent Tekulve	716	Rick Leach
685	Jerry Hairston	717	Ed Vande Berg
686	Doyle Alexander	718	Steve Carlton
687	Alan Trammell	719	Tom Hume
688	Juan Beniquez	720	Richard Dotson
689	Darrell Porter	721	Tom Herr
690	Dane Iorg	722	Bob Knepper
691	Dave Parker	723	Brett Butler
692	Frank White	724	Greg Minton

1987 BASEBALL
CHECKLIST 661-792

792

1951
TOPPS CONNIE MACK
ALL-STARS

The series of 11 die-cut cards which comprise this set is one of Topps' most distinctive and fragile card designs. Printed on thin cardboard, these elegant cards were protected in the wrapper by panels accompanying "Red Backs," but once removed were easily damaged. (They were intended to be folded and used as toy figures). Cards without tops have a value less than one-half of that listed below.

Value of Complete Set in Mint Condition

1.	Alexander, Grover	$300.00
2.	Cochrane, Mickey	$200.00
3.	Collins, Ed	$120.00
4.	Collins, Jimmy	$ 90.00
5.	Gehrig, Lou	$700.00
6.	Johnson, Walter	$400.00
7.	Mack, Connie	$200.00
8.	Mathewson, Christy	$200.00
9.	Ruth, Babe	$700.00
10.	Speaker, Tris	$120.00
11.	Wagner, Honus	$200.00

From: *The Sport Americana Baseball Card Price Guide* 9th Edition by Dr. James Beckett: Copyright © 1987 Published by The Edgewater Book Company Inc.

Cards photographed from the collection of Barry Halper.

CONNIE MACK
MANAGER
Birth Date December 23, 1862
Connie Mack

GROVER CLEVELAND ALEXANDER
1887   PITCHER   1950
G.C. Alexander
CONNIE MACK'S
ALL-TIME ALL-STAR TEAM

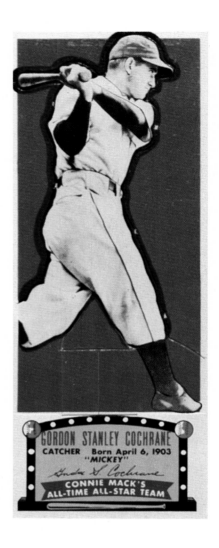

GORDON STANLEY COCHRANE
CATCHER   Born April 6, 1903
"MICKEY"
Gordon S. Cochrane
CONNIE MACK'S
ALL-TIME ALL-STAR TEAM

EDWARD TROWBRIDGE COLLINS
SECOND BASE   Born May 2, 1887
Eddie Collins
CONNIE MACK'S
ALL-TIME ALL-STAR TEAM

JAMES J. COLLINS
1873   THIRD BASE   1943
"JIMMY"
James J. Collins
CONNIE MACK'S
ALL-TIME ALL-STAR TEAM

HENRY LOUIS GEHRIG
1903   FIRST BASE   1941
"THE IRON HORSE"
Lou Gehrig
CONNIE MACK'S
ALL-TIME ALL-STAR TEAM

WALTER JOHNSON
1887   PITCHER   1946
"THE BIG TRAIN"
Walter Johnson
CONNIE MACK'S
ALL-TIME ALL-STAR TEAM

CHRISTOPHER MATHEWSON
1880   PITCHER   1925
"MATTY"
Christy Mathewson
CONNIE MACK'S
ALL-TIME ALL-STAR TEAM

GEORGE HERMAN RUTH
1894   OUTFIELD   1948
Babe Ruth
CONNIE MACK'S
ALL-TIME ALL-STAR TEAM

TRISTAM E. SPEAKER
OUTFIELD   Born April 4, 1888
"GREY EAGLE"
Tris Speaker
CONNIE MACK'S
ALL-TIME ALL-STAR TEAM

JOHN PETER WAGNER
SHORTSTOP   Born Feb. 24, 1874
J. Hons Wagner
CONNIE MACK'S
ALL-TIME ALL-STAR TEAM

Pitching Record & Index

PLAYER	G	IP	W	L	R	ER	SO	BB	GS	CG	SHO	SV	ERA
AASE, DON 87/766	325	956.2	61	54	428	398	552	371	91	22	5	75	3.74
ACKER, JIM 87/407	175	411	20	20	207	182	188	154	27	0	0	12	3.99
AGOSTO, JUAN 87/277	171	190.1	9	10	104	93	110	86	1	0	0	16	4.40
AGUILERA, RICK 87/103	49	264	20	14	119	105	178	73	39	4	0	0	3.58
ALEXANDER, DOYLE 87/686	467	2708.1	160	135	1228	1117	1199	803	370	82	13	3	3.71
ALLEN, NEIL 86/2T, 87/113	367	793.2	53	58	356	322	508	344	46	7	5	75	3.65
ANDERSEN, LARRY 87/503	289	452	12	15	217	187	251	142	1	0	0	14	3.72
ANDERSON, ALLAN 87/336	21	84.1	3	6	54	52	51	30	10	1	0	0	5.55
ANDERSON, RICK 87/594	15	49.2	2	1	17	15	21	11	5	0	0	1	2.72
ANDUJAR, JOAQUIN 86/3T, 87/775	369	2014	122	108	869	781	965	684	282	67	19	9	3.49
AQUINO, LUIS 87/301	7	11.1	1	1	8	8	5	3	0	0	0	0	6.35
ASSENMACHER, PAUL 86/4T, 87/132	61	68.1	7	3	23	19	56	26	0	0	0	7	2.50
ATHERTON, KEITH 87/52	202	374	19	28	171	165	242	150	0	0	0	19	3.97
BAILES, SCOTT 86/5T, 87/585	62	112.2	10	10	70	62	60	43	10	0	0	7	4.95
BAMBERGER, GEORGE 87/468	10	14	0	0	-	-	3	10	1	0	0	1	9.64
BANKHEAD, SCOTT 87/508	24	121	8	9	66	62	94	37	17	0	0	0	4.61
BANNISTER, FLOYD 87/737	300	1832.1	101	117	908	820	1405	680	284	49	14	0	4.03
BEATTIE, JIM 87/191	203	1148.2	52	87	581	532	660	461	182	31	7	1	4.17
BEDROSIAN, STEVE 86/7T, 87/736	294	662.1	42	45	266	241	543	301	46	0	0	70	3.27
BERENGUER, JUAN 86/9T, 87/303	183	645	30	41	324	287	498	335	86	5	2	5	4.00
BERENYI, BRUCE 87/582	142	782	44	55	392	350	607	425	131	13	5	0	4.03
BEST, KARL 87/439	50	79.1	5	6	39	33	64	32	0	0	0	5	3.74
BIELECKI, MIKE 86/10T, 87/394	47	198.2	8	14	113	100	106	114	34	0	0	0	4.53
BIRKBECK, MIKE 87/229	7	2250	1	1	12	13	13	12	4	0	0	0	4.50
BLACK, BUD 87/669	172	834.1	46	50	382	344	428	246	110	16	3	1	3.71
BLUE, VIDA 87/260	502	3344	209	161	1357	1211	2175	1185	473	143	37	2	3.26
BLYLEVEN, BERT 87/25	541	3988	229	197	1532	1365	3090	1072	535	216	54	0	3.08
BODDICKER, MIKE 87/455	136	900.2	63	49	409	360	584	315	126	42	11	0	3.60
BORDI, RICH 86/14T, 87/638	155	330.2	17	18	162	147	218	104	14	0	0	10	4.00
BOSIO, CHRIS 87/448	10	34.2	0	4	27	27	29	13	4	0	0	0	7.01
BOYD, DENNIS 87/285	112	791.1	47	44	376	339	462	190	105	38	6	0	3.86
BROWN, MIKE 87/271	60	253.1	12	20	182	160	115	102	42	3	1	0	5.68
BROWNING, TOM 87/65	80	528	35	22	238	210	316	148	80	10	6	0	3.58
BRYDEN, T.R. 87/387	16	34.1	2	1	25	25	25	21	0	0	0	0	6.55
BURKE, TIM 87/624	146	221.2	18	11	69	65	169	90	2	0	0	12	2.64
BUTCHER, JOHN 87/107	164	833.2	36	49	444	409	363	229	113	23	6	6	4.42
CALHOUN, JEFF 87/282	73	105..2	3	6	40	31	72	38	0	0	0	4	2.64
CAMACHO, ERNIE 87/353	138	200	7	16	85	80	108	91	3	0	0	43	3.60
CAMPBELL, BILL 86/17T, 87/674	693	1219.2	83	68	538	475	860	491	9	2	1	126	3.51
CANDELARIA, JOHN 87/630	350	2016.2	141	89	775	698	1276	477	300	47	11	15	3.12
CANDIOTTI, TOM 86/18T, 87/463	54	340.1	22	18	154	139	211	132	48	19	4	0	3.68
CARLTON, STEVE 87/718	705	5054.2	323	229	2000	1749	4040	1742	687	251	55	1	3.11
CARMAN, DON 87/355	133	235	19	10	84	76	201	96	14	2	1	9	2.91
CARY, CHUCK 87/171	38	55.1	1	3	27	21	43	23	0	0	0	2	3.42
CAUDILL, BILL 87/733	439	659.1	35	52	289	265	612	287	24	0	0	105	3.62
CERUTTI, JOHN 86/23T, 87/557	38	152	9	6	80	71	94	51	21	2	1	1	4.20
CLANCY, JIM 87/122	279	1768.1	102	116	895	812	939	687	277	64	10	0	4.13
CLEAR, MARK 86/25T, 87/640	394	689.1	62	44	332	291	691	469	0	0	0	77	3.80
CLEMENS, ROGER 87/1, 87/340	69	485.2	40	13	182	170	438	133	68	18	3	0	3.15
CLEMENTS, PAT 87/16	133	157.1	5	6	57	56	67	72	0	0	0	5	3.20
CLUTTERBUCK, BRYAN 87/562	20	56.2	0	1	32	27	38	16	0	0	0	0	4.29
COCANOWER, JAIME 87/423	79	365.2	16	25	208	162	139	201	47	5	1	0	3.99
CODIROLI, CHRIS 87/217	121	629.1	38	40	369	321	288	226	101	13	2	2	4.59
CONROY, TIM 86/28T, 87/338	125	426.1	15	30	253	219	285	259	62	5	1	0	4.62
CORBETT, DOUG 87/359	302	530	24	28	206	184	327	187	1	0	0	65	3.12
CORREA, ED 87/334	37	212.2	13	14	111	103	199	137	33	4	2	0	4.36
COWLEY, JOE 86/29T, 87/27	90	457.2	33	21	217	199	327	215	72	8	1	0	3.91
COX, DANNY 87/621	108	700.1	42	39	295	248	345	201	106	19	5	0	3.19
CRAIG, ROGER 87/193	368	1537	74	98	-	-	803	522	186	58	7	19	3.82
CRAWFORD, STEVE 87/589	144	309.1	14	12	162	133	152	94	16	2	0	17	3.87
DARLING, RON 87/75	108	726	44	24	285	252	510	316	107	11	6	0	3.12
DARWIN, DANNY 87/157	295	1241	72	78	571	490	789	400	141	38	7	17	3.55
DAVIS, JOEL 86/30T, 87/299	31	176.2	7	8	98	88	91	77	30	2	0	0	4.48
DAVIS, MARK 87/21	221	534.1	22	44	285	260	462	208	60	3	2	11	4.38
DAVIS, RON 87/383	447	692.1	46	52	324	303	550	276	0	0	0	130	3.94
DAVIS, STORM 87/349	154	855	54	40	378	347	486	282	121	27	4	1	3.65
DAWLEY, BILL 87/54	203	356.1	22	20	123	114	221	122	0	0	0	23	2.88
DAYLEY, KEN 87/59	139	303.2	14	26	169	141	309	104	33	0	0	16	4.18
DEDMON, JEFF 87/373	176	270.2	16	12	140	112	153	123	0	0	0	7	3.72
DELEON, JOSE 87/421	98	558.1	21	43	261	240	499	287	82	10	3	4	3.87
DENNY, JOHN 86/32T, 87/644	325	2149.2	123	108	967	1146	1146	778	322	62	18	0	3.58
DESHAIES, JIM 87/2, 87/167	30	154	12	6	67	61	135	66	28	1	1	0	3.56
DIPINO, FRANK 87/662	233	333.1	15	29	162	141	279	143	6	0	0	43	3.81
DIXON, KEN 87/528	71	377.1	19	18	185	175	286	151	53	5	1	1	4.17
DOTSON, RICHARD 87/720	206	1294.2	83	76	639	577	704	510	202	42	9	0	4.01
DOWNS, KELLY 87/438	14	88.1	4	4	29	27	64	30	14	1	0	0	2.75
DRABEK, DOUG 87/283	27	131.2	7	8	64	60	76	50	21	0	0	0	4.10
DRAVECKY, DAVE 87/470	169	821.1	50	43	315	279	396	239	109	22	6	10	3.06
ECKERSLEY, DENNIS 87/459	376	2496	151	128	1101	1018	1627	624	359	100	20	3	3.67
EICHHORN, MARK 86/34T, 87/371	76	195	14	9	60	53	182	59	7	0	0	10	2.45
FARR, STEVE 86/35T, 87/473	103	263	13	16	115	110	202	105	19	0	0	10	3.76
FERNANDEZ, SID 87/570	75	470.2	31	22	182	172	451	212	73	5	1	1	3.29
FINLEY, CHUCK 87/446	25	46.1	3	1	17	17	37	23	0	0	0	0	3.30
FIREOVID, STEVE 87/357	28	64.2	2	1	26	24	27	15	5	0	0	0	3.34
FISHER, BRIAN 87/316	117	195	13	9	93	79	152	66	0	0	0	20	3.65
FLANAGAN, MIKE 87/748	328	2090	136	103	966	892	1175	656	311	94	17	1	3.84
FONTENOT, RAY 87/124	145	493.2	25	26	253	221	216	153	62	3	1	2	4.03
FORSCH, BOB 87/257	392	2371.1	143	116	1088	954	950	697	359	64	17	3	3.62
FORSTER, TERRY 86/37T, 87/652	614	1105.1	54	65	454	397	791	457	39	5	0	127	3.23
FRANCO, JOHN 87/305	195	279.1	24	11	95	80	200	120	0	0	0	45	2.58
FRAZIER, GEORGE 87/207	361	594.1	30	38	300	270	391	262	0	0	0	27	4.09
GARBER, GENE 87/351	843	1393.1	88	99	595	509	869	403	9	4	0	194	3.29
GARRETS, SCOTT 87/475	154	360	26	20	149	127	283	187	26	3	1	23	320
GOODEN, DWIGHT 87/130	99	744.2	58	19	215	189	744	222	99	35	13	0	2.28
GOSSAGE, RICH 87/380	725	1482.1	101	89	531	473	1275	592	37	16	0	278	2.87
GROSS, KEVIN 87/163	136	672.1	39	36	313	283	455	254	98	15	5	1	3.79
GUANTE, CECILIO 87/219	201	355.2	13	17	139	121	293	136	0	0	0	20	3.06
GUBICZA, MARK 87/326	93	547	36	30	255	238	328	236	81	7	4	0	3.92
GUETTERMAN, LEE 87/307	44	80.1	0	4	69	64	40	32	4	1	0	0	7.17
GUIDRY, RON 87/375	334	2219.1	163	80	875	800	1650	580	296	93	26	4	3.24
GULLICKSON, BILL 86/42T, 87/489	213	1430.2	87	73	597	545	799	348	207	37	8	0	3.43
GUMPERT, DAVE 87/487	78	116.1	3	2	61	52	63	44	1	0	0	5	4.02
GUZMAN, JOSE 86/43T, 87/363	34	205	12	17	114	97	111	74	34	2	0	0	4.36
HAAS, MOOSE 86/44T, 87/413	257	1614.2	98	81	777	712	840	427	243	56	8	2	3.97
HAMMAKER, ATLEE 87/781	97	590	30	32	258	226	364	128	91	13	5	0	3.45
HARRIS, GREG 87/44	216	440	22	25	188	167	373	178	25	1	0	35	3.42
HAVENS, BRAD 87/398	109	438	21	31	257	240	267	171	58	6	2	1	4.93
HAWKINS, ANDY 87/183	142	767.1	43	37	372	324	347	287	119	15	5	0	3.80
HENKE, TOM 87/510	132	191.1	15	9	80	71	211	72	0	0	0	43	3.34
HERNANDEZ, WILLIE 87/515	604	897	59	52	359	329	669	282	11	0	0	114	3..30
HERSHISER, OREL 87/385	124	668.2	44	25	255	212	465	210	89	25	10	3	2.85
HESKETH, JOE 87/189	51	283	18	12	110	98	212	91	45	3	2	1	3.12
HIGUERA, TEDDY 87/250	66	460.2	35	19	189	169	334	137	64	22	6	0	3.30
HONEYCUTT, RICK 87/753	275	1562.1	87	105	750	673	649	453	244	46	10	1	3.76

Pitching Record & Index

PLAYER	G	IP	W	L	R	ER	SO	BB	GS	CG	SHO	SV	ERA
HORTON, RICKY (87/542)	128	315.2	16	9	108	102	184	99	30	2	1	5	2.91
HOUGH, CHARLIE (87/70)	609	2168.2	131	115	963	854	1383	918	193	65	10	61	3.54
HOWELL, JAY (87/391)	202	390	26	26	184	172	312	146	21	2	0	52	3.97
HOWELL, KEN (87/477)	150	235	15	24	110	97	243	107	1	0	0	30	3.71
HOYT, LAMARR (87/275)	244	1311.1	98	68	637	582	681	279	172	48	8	10	3.99
HUDSON, CHARLES (87/191)	127	680	32	42	353	301	399	237	105	7	1	0	3.98
HUISMANN, MARK (87/187)	106	221.2	9	8	109	99	155	66	1	0	0	8	4.02
HUME, TOM (86/47T, 87/719)	494	1002.1	55	67	467	415	503	341	49	5	0	92	3.73
HURST, BRUCE (87/705)	171	1004	55	54	525	481	687	338	152	32	9	0	4.31
JACKSON, ROY LEE (87/138)	280	559.1	28	34	260	234	351	203	18	1	0	34	3.77
JAMES, BOB (87/342)	236	353	20	20	162	144	306	140	2	0	0	63	3.67
JOHN, TOMMY (87/236)	682	4279.2	264	210	1781	1536	2083	1144	625	159	45	4	3.23
JOHNSON, JOHN HENRY (87/377)	204	577	26	32	264	233	389	232	59	9	2	9	3.63
JONES, BARRY (87/494)	26	37.1	3	4	16	12	29	21	0	0	0	3	2.89
KERFELD, CHARLIE (86/52T, 87/145)	72	138	15	4	54	47	107	67	6	0	0	7	3.07
KEY, JIMMY (87/29)	134	506.2	32	22	212	195	270	156	67	7	2	10	3.46
KING, ERIC (86/53T, 87/36)	33	138.1	11	4	54	54	79	63	16	3	1	3	3.51
KIPPER, BOB (86/54T, 87/289)	27	142	7	11	84	73	94	44	24	0	0	0	4.63
KNEPPER, BOB (87/722)	338	2145.2	114	118	944	819	1206	642	322	73	27	1	3.44
KRUEGER, BILL (87/238)	86	437.1	27	29	269	218	185	220	66	5	0	1	4.49
KRUKOW, MIKE (87/580)	311	1859.1	108	104	900	794	1281	672	299	37	10	1	3.84
LACOSS, MIKE (86/57T, 87/151)	281	1179	61	67	614	536	487	487	163	21	7	6	4.09
LADD, PETE (86/58T, 87/572)	205	286.2	17	23	147	132	209	96	1	0	0	39	4.14
LAHTI, JEFF (87/367)	205	286	17	11	109	99	137	111	1	0	0	20	3.12
LAMP, DENNIS (87/768)	396	1353.2	74	76	670	587	590	411	157	21	7	33	3.90
LANGSTON, MARK (87/215)	96	591	36	38	326	291	521	332	93	16	2	0	4.43
LAPOINT, DAVE (86/61T, 87/754)	191	898.2	46	49	453	396	532	358	131	5	2	1	3.97
LEARY, TIM (86/64T, 87/32)	61	288	17	20	153	131	180	84	45	4	2	0	4.09
LEFFERTS, CRAIG (87/501)	261	385.2	22	22	139	124	236	127	5	0	0	17	2.89
LEIBRANDT, CHARLIE (87/223)	173	928.1	58	44	429	389	375	288	132	22	7	2	3.77
LEIPER, DAVE (87/441)	41	38.2	3	2	24	24	18	23	0	0	0	1	5.59
LEONARD, DENNIS (86/65T, 87/38)	312	2187.1	144	106	1008	898	1323	622	302	103	23	1	3.69
LOLLAR, TIM (87/396)	199	906	47	52	459	430	600	480	131	9	4	4	4.27
LOPEZ, AURELIO (87/659)	433	872.1	60	35	370	341	614	355	9	0	0	92	3.52
LOYND, MIKE (87/126)	9	42	2	2	30	25	33	19	8	0	0	1	5.36
LUCAS, GARY (87/696)	361	594.1	28	39	233	194	366	192	18	0	0	60	2.94
LUGO, URBANO (87/92)	26	104.1	4	5	45	43	51	35	13	1	0	0	3.71
LYNCH, ED (87/697)	190	829.1	45	45	396	352	316	181	111	8	2	4	3.82
MADDUX, MIKE (87/553)	16	78	3	7	56	47	44	34	16	0	0	0	5.42
MAHLER, MICKEY (86/68T)	122	406	14	32	242	211	262	190	58	3	1	4	4.68
MAHLER, RICK (87/242)	216	1084	61	59	512	464	529	361	154	28	5	2	3.85
MARTINEZ, DENNY (87/252)	338	1873.1	111	99	951	870	921	611	258	70	11	5	4.18
MARTINEZ, TIPPY (87/728)	543	831	55	42	348	312	629	420	2	0	0	115	3.38
MASON, MIKE (87/646)	110	532	25	35	282	255	307	195	80	7	2	0	4.31
MASON, ROGER (86/70T, 87/526)	21	111.2	5	8	59	50	84	51	18	2	1	1	4.03
MATHEWS, GREG (87/567)	23	145.1	11	8	61	59	67	44	22	1	0	0	3.65
MCCASKILL, KIRK (87/194)	64	436	29	22	203	191	304	156	62	16	3	0	3.94
MCCLURE, BOB (86/71T, 87/707)	424	924	48	48	438	396	557	408	73	12	1	41	3.86
MCCULLERS, LANCE (87/559)	91	171	10	12	61	51	119	74	7	0	0	10	2.68
MCDOWELL, ROGER (87/185)	137	255.1	20	14	91	83	135	79	2	0	0	39	2.93
MCGAFFIGAN, ANDY (86/72T, 87/742)	142	455.1	20	23	188	174	343	151	51	3	1	5	3.44
MCGREGOR, SCOTT (87/708)	326	2038.2	136	98	944	869	855	476	290	82	22	5	3.84
MCMURTY, CRAIG (87/461)	127	532.2	25	35	268	240	282	260	76	6	3	1	4.06
MCWILLIAMS, LARRY (87/564)	258	1240.1	68	67	598	539	772	424	184	29	11	2	3.91
MINTON, GREG (87/724)	537	847.1	44	52	352	303	343	366	7	0	0	124	3.22
MOHORCIC, DALE (87/497)	58	79	2	4	25	22	29	15	0	0	0	7	2.51
MOONEYHAM, BILL (87/548)	45	99.2	4	5	53	50	75	67	6	0	0	2	4.52
MOORE, DONNIE (87/115)	375	596.1	36	36	276	241	377	165	4	0	0	80	3.64
MOORE, MIKE (87/727)	157	997.1	48	62	534	492	640	388	152	35	6	1	4.44
MORGAN, MIKE (87/546)	101	507	21	45	302	277	228	237	78	14	1	1	4.92
MORRIS, JACK (87/778)	302	2122.1	144	94	910	842	1327	754	280	110	19	0	3.57
MOYER, JAMIE (87/227)	16	87.1	7	4	52	49	45	42	16	1	1	0	5.05
MULHOLLAND, TERRY (87/536)	15	54.2	1	7	33	30	27	35	10	0	0	0	4.94
MURPHY, ROB (87/82)	36	53.1	6	0	6	6	37	23	0	0	0	1	1.01
MYERS, RANDY (87/213)	11	12.2	0	0	5	5	15	10	0	0	0	0	3.55
NELSON, GENE (87/273)	160	528.2	28	34	287	267	305	229	59	6	1	9	4.55
NIEDENFUER, TOM (87/538)	295	424	29	28	136	130	340	136	0	0	0	63	2.76
NIEKRO, JOE (87/344)	670	3426	213	190	1506	1331	1656	1191	472	106	29	16	3.50
NIEKRO, PHIL (86/77T, 87/694)	838	5265	311	261	2238	1915	3278	1743	690	243	45	29	3.27
NIELSEN, SCOTT (87/57)	10	56	4	4	29	25	20	12	9	2	2	0	4.02
NIEMANN, RANDY (86/78T, 87/147)	116	194.2	6	8	107	98	101	75	10	3	2	3	4.53
NIEVES, JUAN (86/79T, 87/79)	35	184.2	11	12	124	102	116	77	33	4	3	0	4.97
NIPPER, AL (87/617)	83	519.2	31	31	281	251	253	188	77	15	0	0	4.35
NOLES, DICKIE (87/244)	229	789.2	32	48	447	400	421	310	93	3	3	7	4.56
NUNEZ, ED (87/427)	143	252	11	13	116	105	194	98	11	0	0	23	3.75
O'NEAL, RANDY (87/196)	69	235.2	10	3	118	100	132	86	26	2	0	3	3.82
OELKERS, BRYAN (87/77)	45	103.1	3	8	72	69	46	57	12	0	0	1	6.01
OJEDA, BOB (86/81T, 87/746)	172	935.2	62	44	435	398	573	337	143	27	7	1	3.83
OLWINE, ED (87/159)	37	47.2	0	0	20	18	37	17	0	0	0	1	3.40
ONTIVEROS, STEVE (87/161)	85	147.1	3	5	57	54	90	44	0	0	0	18	3.30
OROSCO, JESSE (87/704)	314	518.1	44	38	166	143	428	209	4	0	0	91	2.48
PALMER, DAVE (86/84T, 87/324)	157	787.1	49	36	335	294	540	311	121	9	3	2	3.36
PASTORE, FRANK (86/85T, 87/576)	220	986.1	48	58	507	470	541	301	139	22	7	6	4.29
PENA, ALEJANDRO (87/787)	131	511.1	26	21	211	178	337	162	65	12	7	4	3.13
PERRY, PAT (87/417)	52	81	3	3	31	29	35	37	0	0	0	2	3.22
PETRY, DAN (87/752)	227	1504.1	98	74	675	599	773	572	224	47	10	0	3.58
PLESAC, DAN (86/87T, 87/279)	51	91	10	7	34	30	75	29	0	0	0	14	2.97
PLUNK, ERIC (87/587)	26	120.1	4	7	75	71	98	102	15	0	0	0	5.31
PORTUGAL, MARK (87/419)	33	137	7	13	72	69	79	64	21	3	0	1	4.53
POWELL, DENNIS (87/47)	43	94.2	3	8	51	48	50	38	8	0	0	1	4.56
POWER, TED (87/437)	264	476.1	34	29	218	197	297	222	22	1	0	41	3.72
PRICE, JOE (87/332)	226	659.2	36	31	292	261	450	239	75	10	1	8	3.56
PULIDO, AL (87/642)	12	34.2	1	1	22	20	16	11	4	0	0	1	5.19
QUISENBERRY, DAN (87/714)	506	845.1	47	42	267	236	295	124	0	0	0	229	2.51
RASMUSSEN, DENNIS (87/555)	81	465	30	17	231	210	317	184	72	6	1	0	4.06
RAWLEY, SHANE (87/771)	374	1298	81	79	599	548	713	510	137	32	5	40	3..80
REARDON, JEFF (87/165)	456	665.2	42	46	226	207	537	246	0	0	0	162	2.80
REED, JERRY (87/619)	68	157.2	9	7	89	77	80	53	10	0	0	8	4.40
REUSCHEL, RICK (87/521)	436	2771.2	162	155	1195	1056	1652	759	414	81	20	4	3.43
REUSS, JERRY (87/682)	537	3218.2	194	163	1438	1251	1744	1018	468	123	37	11	3.50
RHODEN, RICK (87/365)	333	2118	121	97	903	818	1177	643	304	60	16	1	3.48
RIGHETTI, DAVE (87/5, 87/40)	294	832	58	44	312	278	699	340	76	13	2	107	3.01
RIJO, JOSE (87/34)	75	319.2	17	23	182	158	288	169	40	4	0	3	4.45
ROBINSON, DON (87/712)	301	1137	59	63	538	487	772	419	126	22	3	31	3.85
ROBINSON, JEFF (86/93T, 87/389)	106	288.1	13	18	156	133	200	94	34	1	1	8	4.15
ROBINSON, RON (87/119)	115	264.2	18	12	115	102	217	88	17	1	0	15	3.47
ROMANICK, RON (87/136)	82	531	31	29	276	250	189	167	82	15	4	0	4.24
RUFFIN, BRUCE (87/499)	21	146.1	9	4	53	40	70	44	21	6	0	0	2.46
RUHLE, VERN (87/221)	327	1410.2	67	88	675	585	582	348	188	29	12	11	3.73
RUSSELL, JEFF (87/444)	93	394	18	31	222	192	239	145	53	6	2	4	4.39
RYAN, NOLAN (87/757)	611	4115.1	253	226	1643	1440	4277	2268	577	203	54	3	3.15
SABERHAGEN, BRET (87/140)	100	549	37	29	227	208	343	103	75	16	4	1	3.41
SAMBITO, JOE (86/97T, 87/451)	414	590.2	35	32	212	183	454	179	5	1	1	84	2.79
SANDERSON, SCOTT (87/534)	229	1313.2	78	69	551	497	883	328	207	30	9	3	3.40

Pitching Record & Index

PLAYER	G	IP	W	L	R	ER	SO	BB	GS	CG	SHO	SV	ERA
SCHATZEDER, DAN 87/789	328	1077	58	59	473	429	584	378	118	18	4	6	3.58
SCHERRER, BILL 87/98	193	267.2	7	8	127	115	177	119	2	0	0	11	3.87
SCHIRALDI, CALVIN 87/94	40	94.2	6	5	48	45	92	36	7	0	0	9	4.28
SCHMIDT, DAVE 86/99T, 87/703	221	436.1	23	28	179	154	270	119	14	1	1	34	3.18
SCHROM, KEN 86/100T, 87/635	144	746.1	45	38	409	370	311	263	108	18	2	1	4.46
SCHULZE, DON 87/297	62	281.2	11	21	191	171	119	88	49	4	0	0	5.46
SCOTT, MIKE 87/330	212	1160	65	62	541	477	750	363	185	16	10	3	3.70
SCURRY, ROD 87/665	293	429.2	19	30	174	152	398	256	7	0	0	37	3.18
SEARAGE, RAY 87/149	126	164.1	5	6	66	62	117	85	0	0	0	9	3.40
SEAVER, TOM 86/101T, 87/425	656	4782	311	205	1674	1511	3640	1390	647	231	61	1	2.84
SEBRA, BOB 87/479	24	111.2	5	7	56	53	79	39	17	3	1	0	4.27
SELLERS, JEFF 87/12	18	104.1	5	7	66	54	57	47	17	2	0	0	4.66
SHIRLEY, BOB 87/524	419	1390.1	66	94	657	579	777	521	161	16	2	18	3.75
SHOW, ERIC 87/730	188	949.2	62	46	385	348	569	375	136	16	7	6	3.30
SISK, DOUG 87/404	208	334.1	14	15	142	112	126	188	0	0	0	30	3.01
SLATON, JIM 87/432	496	2683.2	151	158	1335	1202	1191	1004	360	86	22	14	4.03
SMITH, BRYN 87/505	193	836.1	49	41	356	304	493	224	103	14	7	6	3.27
SMITH, DAVE 87/50	361	526.2	38	29	177	153	337	181	1	0	0	100	2.61
SMITH, LEE 87/23	396	598.1	36	41	210	192	548	232	6	0	0	144	2.89
SMITH, ZANE 87/544	83	371.2	18	26	186	159	240	198	53	5	3	1	3.85
SMITHSON, MIKE 87/225	148	977	56	59	598	455	544	273	147	39	5	0	4.19
SNELL, NATE 87/86	82	180.1	6	4	82	63	71	53	0	0	0	5	3.14
SOFF, RAY 87/671	30	38.1	4	2	17	14	22	13	0	0	0	0	3.29
SOTO, MARIO 87/517	277	1611.1	94	83	665	604	1404	617	204	69	12	4	3.37
SPECK, CLIFF 87/269	13	28.1	2	1	13	13	21	15	1	0	0	0	4.13
ST CLAIRE, RANDY 87/467	57	95.2	7	3	41	39	50	34	0	0	0	1	3.67
STANLEY, BOB 87/175	503	1374.1	100	76	606	52?	537	374	65	17	6	123	3.44
STEWART, DAVE 87/14	247	766	39	40	367	337	484	310	72	9	1	19	3.96
STEWART, SAMMY 86/103T, 87/204	334	929.2	55	46	399	365	561	481	25	4	1	42	3.53
STIEB, DAVE 87/90	259	1859.1	102	92	773	690	1069	631	254	85	21	1	3.34
STODDARD, TIM 87/788	386	560.1	35	30	257	238	459	292	0	0	0	65	3.82
SUTCLIFFE, RICK 87/142	251	1416.2	86	68	669	605	934	599	191	41	12	6	3.84
SUTTER, BRUCE 87/435	623	955.1	67	67	344	304	821	298	0	0	0	286	2.75
SUTTON, DON 87/673	723	5002.2	310	239	1959	1776	3431	1272	706	177	58	5	3.20
SWIFT, BILL 87/67	52	236	8	19	156	134	110	103	38	1	0	0	5.11
SWINDELL, GREG 87/319	9	61.2	5	2	35	29	46	15	9	1	0	0	4.23
TANANA, FRANK 87/726	408	2758.1	159	153	1180	1041	1925	772	392	123	28	0	3.40
TEKULVE, KENT 87/684	853	1199.1	85	76	419	358	645	417	0	0	0	176	2.69
TERRELL, WALT 87/72	125	816	49	45	391	353	404	342	123	21	8	0	3.89
TERRY, SCOTT 87/453	28	55.2	1	2	40	38	32	32	3	0	0	0	6.14
TEWKSBURY, BOB 86/110T, 87/254	23	130.1	9	5	58	48	49	31	20	2	0	0	3.31
THIGPEN, BOBBY 87/61	20	35.2	2	0	7	7	20	12	0	0	0	7	1.77
THURMOND, MARK 87/361	131	554.2	35	30	251	216	212	176	89	6	3	5	3.50
TIBBS, JAY 86/114T, 87/9	84	509	23	27	241	211	255	186	79	11	5	0	3.73
TOLVER, FRED 87/63	19	60.2	0	6	31	24	47	35	9	0	0	1	3.56
TROUT, STEVE 87/750	242	1294	74	75	648	567	566	466	200	29	7	4	3.94
TRUJILLO, MIKE 87/402	41	131	7	6	72	62	42	44	11	2	1	2	4.26
TUDOR, JOHN 87/110	204	1342.2	85	58	544	487	775	366	192	44	14	1	3.26
VALENZUELA, FERNANDO 87/410	210	1554.2	99	68	589	507	1274	540	200	84	26	1	2.94
VANDE BERG, ED 86/118T, 87/717	332	409.2	22	26	191	168	256	168	17	2	0	20	3.69
VIOLA, FRANK 87/310	165	1090	63	64	591	530	689	354	164	33	6	0	4.38
VON OHLEN, DAVE 87/287	123	161.2	7	7	67	57	56	60	0	0	0	4	3.17
WADDELL, TOM 87/657	107	209.2	15	10	96	94	112	76	9	1	0	15	4.03
WALK, BOB 86/120T, 87/628	127	573.2	33	32	309	277	326	241	89	7	3	2	4.35
WALTER, GENE 86/121T, 87/248	72	120	2	4	53	47	102	57	0	0	0	4	3.53
WARD, DUANE 87/153	12	18	0	2	17	16	9	12	1	0	0	0	8.00
WEGMAN, BILL 86/123T, 87/179	38	216	7	12	128	120	88	46	35	2	0	0	5.00
WELCH, BOB 87/328	257	1568.1	100	77	608	545	1096	479	232	41	19	8	3.13
WELSH, CHRIS 87/592	122	538	22	31	297	266	192	189	75	8	3	0	4.45
WHITSON, EDDIE 87/155	304	1295.1	69	73	642	573	729	477	189	16	6	8	3.98
WILLIAMS, FRANK 87/96	146	231.2	14	9	96	83	178	107	1	1	1	4	3.22
WILLIAMS, MITCH 86/125T, 87/291	80	98	8	5	39	39	90	79	0	0	0	8	3.58
WILLIS, CARL 87/101	57	91.2	2	6	64	57	37	44	2	0	0	2	5.60
WILLS, FRANK 87/551	66	235	12	19	146	141	143	112	27	1	0	5	5.40
WINN, JIM 87/262	96	193.1	7	11	106	96	106	84	10	0	0	4	4.47
WITT, BOBBY 86/126T, 87/415	31	157.2	11	9	104	96	174	143	31	0	0	0	5.48
WITT, MIKE 87/760	201	1228.1	71	59	540	480	821	424	169	43	8	5	3.52
WOJNA, ED 87/88	22	81	4	6	54	41	37	35	14	1	0	0	4.56
WOODWARD, ROB 87/632	14	62.1	3	3	34	26	30	20	8	0	0	0	3.75
WORRELL, TODD 86/127T, 87/7, 87/465	91	125.1	12	10	36	31	90	48	0	0	0	41	2.23
WRIGHT, RICKY 86/129T, 87/202	55	102.2	3	3	50	49	67	60	7	0	0	0	4.30
YETT, RICH 87/134	40	79	5	3	49	46	50	39	4	1	1	1	5.24
YOUMANS, FLOYD 87/105	47	296	17	15	120	107	256	167	44	6	2	0	3.25
YOUNG, CURT 87/519	76	361.2	22	18	196	178	181	115	53	7	3	0	4.43
YOUNG, MATT 87/19	157	639	37	48	352	309	421	258	94	12	4	14	4.35

Batting Record & Index

PLAYER	G	AB	R	H	2B	3B	HR	RBI	SB	SLG	BB	SO	AVG
AGUAYO, LUIS 87/755	328	561	89	141	23	8	18	67	5	.417	52	95	.251
ALDRETE, MIKE 87/71	84	216	27	54	18	3	2	25	1	.389	33	34	.250
ALLANSON, ANDY 86/1T, 87/436	101	293	30	66	7	3	1	29	10	.280	14	36	.225
ALMON, BILL 87/447	1148	3230	376	826	132	25	36	290	127	.346	238	604	.256
ANDERSON, DAVE 87/73	351	926	118	210	35	4	9	69	31	.302	114	151	.227
ANDERSON, SPARKY 87/218	152	477	42	104	9	3	0	34	6	.249	42	53	.218
ARMAS, TONY 87/535	1224	4513	542	1134	174	35	224	727	16	.454	230	1055	.251
ASHBY, ALAN 87/112	1150	3449	321	835	156	12	69	414	7	.354	375	525	.242
BACKMAN, WALLY 87/48	572	1775	272	506	77	13	6	125	86	.353	194	243	.285
BAILEY, MARK 87/197	279	829	94	188	35	1	23	94	1	.355	148	186	.227
BAINES, HAROLD 87/772	992	3754	492	1077	182	38	140	589	29	.468	263	539	.287
BAKER, DUSTY 87/565	2039	7117	964	1981	320	23	242	1013	137	.432	762	926	.278
BALBONI, STEVE 87/240	493	1750	204	412	81	7	100	276	1	.461	155	512	.235
BANDO, CHRIS 87/322	375	999	108	236	36	2	21	117	1	.339	118	156	.236
BARFIELD, JESSE 87/655	715	2325	371	634	112	19	128	376	45	.502	238	578	.273
BARRATT, MARTY 87/39	494	1696	216	476	89	8	12	163	27	.364	166	108	.281
BASS, KEVIN 87/85	546	1689	219	462	84	18	40	195	48	.416	82	228	.274
BAYLOR, DON 86/6T, 87/230	2072	7546	1141	1982	350	28	315	1179	280	.442	726	966	.263
BEANE, BILLY 87/114	93	201	20	42	7	0	3	16	2	.289	11	59	.209
BELL, BUDDY 87/545	2133	8068	1046	2273	392	53	177	993	50	.409	732	695	.282
BELL, GEORGE 87/681	574	2129	297	610	112	21	92	319	43	.488	117	282	.287
BELLIARD, RAFAEL 87/541	167	354	41	82	5	2	0	32	17	.257	26	61	.232
BENEDICT, BRUCE 87/186	789	2387	187	594	87	6	16	230	12	.310	269	192	.249
BENIQUEZ, JUAN 86/8T, 87/143	1377	4338	581	1193	176	29	70	421	104	.377	325	507	.275
BERGMAN, DAVE 87/700	732	1253	151	310	43	10	26	130	13	.360	179	170	.247
BERNAZARD, TONY 87/758	925	3181	450	841	151	28	61	342	102	.387	373	523	.264
BIANCALANA, BUDDY 87/554	256	479	65	102	15	7	5	23	8	.305	39	135	.213
BILARDELLO, DANN 87/577	298	773	61	163	30	0	16	74	3	.312	52	130	.211
BOCHTE, BRUCE 87/496	1538	5233	643	1478	250	21	100	658	43	.396	653	662	.282
BOCHY, BRUCE 87/428	320	727	67	180	34	2	24	82	1	.399	56	156	.248
BOGGS, WADE 87/150	725	2778	474	978	178	17	32	322	9	.463	417	206	.352
BONDS, BARRY 86/11T, 87/320	113	413	72	92	26	3	16	48	36	.416	65	102	.223
BONILLA, BOBBY 86/12T, 87/184	138	426	55	109	16	4	3	43	8	.333	62	88	.256
BONILLA, JUAN 86/13T, 87/668	398	1391	139	359	46	9	6	96	7	.317	111	99	.258
BOONE, BOB 87/763	1843	5982	557	1501	252	24	96	702	32	.349	533	497	.251
BOROS, STEVE 86/15T, 87/143	422	1255	141	308	50	7	26	149	11	.359	181	174	.245
BOSLEY, THAD 87/58	587	1276	152	353	37	11	17	121	43	.363	119	213	.277
BOSTON, DARYL 87/482	186	514	57	120	27	5	8	40	23	.352	39	97	.233
BRADLEY, PHIL 87/525	449	1556	245	470	74	16	38	167	67	.443	174	329	.302
BRADLEY, SCOTT 87/376	105	290	27	80	11	4	5	31	1	.393	15	13	.276
BRAGGS, GLENN 87/622	58	215	19	51	8	2	4	18	1	.349	11	47	.237
BRANTLEY, MICKEY 87/347	27	102	12	20	3	2	3	7	1	.353	10	21	.196
BREAM, SID 87/35	246	730	93	185	47	5	22	106	14	.422	86	108	.253
BRENLY, BOB 87/125	615	1924	242	489	88	5	67	251	33	.410	240	289	.254
BRETT, GEORGE 87/400	1741	6675	1072	2095	428	112	209	1050	141	.505	695	488	.314
BROCK, GREG 87/26	496	1506	195	351	53	2	71	219	19	.412	214	255	.233
BROOKENS, TOM 87/713	927	2658	324	657	124	30	48	300	74	.371	179	416	.247
BROOKS, HUBBIE 87/650	787	2954	313	822	137	23	55	377	38	.396	187	464	.278
BROWN, CHRIS 87/180	270	932	113	273	43	6	24	121	17	.429	80	140	.293
BROWN, MIKE 87/341	297	853	101	228	47	7	23	110	5	.420	76	123	.267
BRUNANSKY, TOM 87/776	758	2765	369	687	131	11	133	384	25	.448	321	484	.248
BUCKNER, BILL 87/764	2176	8424	1008	2464	462	46	164	1072	175	.417	402	395	.292
BUECHELE, STEVE 87/176	222	680	76	160	25	5	24	75	8	.393	49	136	.235
BURLESON, RICK 86/16T, 87/579	1284	4933	630	1358	242	22	48	435	72	.362	403	447	.275
BUSH, RANDY 87/364	519	1394	178	343	79	15	43	192	9	.417	136	232	.246
BUTERA, SAL 87/358	280	619	52	147	17	2	5	56	0	.296	77	54	.237
BUTLER, BRETT 87/723	752	2695	442	747	95	53	17	198	200	.371	217	277	.277
CABELL, ENOS 87/509	1688	5952	753	1647	263	56	60	596	238	.370	259	691	.277
CANGELOSI, JOHN 86/19T, 87/201	142	440	67	103	16	3	2	32	50	.298	71	62	.234
CANSECO, JOSE 86/20T, 87/620	186	696	101	173	32	1	38	130	16	.461	69	206	.249
CARTER, GARY 87/20	1689	6063	847	1646	287	26	271	999	36	.461	680	763	.271
CARTER, JOE 87/220	394	1447	210	404	70	11	57	222	56	.461	68	238	.279
CASTILLO, CARMEN 86/21T, 87/513	309	756	117	192	29	4	32	107	7	.430	51	142	.254
CERONE, RICK 86/22T, 87/129	858	2796	266	665	126	12	43	304	4	.338	198	290	.238
CEY, RON 87/767	2028	7058	965	1845	322	21	312	1128	24	.446	990	1203	.261
CHAMBLISS, CHRIS 87/777	2174	7570	912	2109	392	42	185	972	40	.415	632	925	.279
CLARK, JACK 87/520	1235	4405	702	1213	235	35	194	705	62	.477	625	705	.275
CLARK, WILL 86/24T, 87/420	111	408	66	117	27	2	11	41	4	.444	34	76	.287
CLEMENTE, ROBERTO 87/313	2433	9454	1416	3000	400	166	240	1305	83	.475	621	1230	.317
COLEMAN, VINCE 87/590	305	1236	201	309	33	18	1	69	217	.308	110	213	.250
COLES, DARNELL 86/26T, 87/411	244	815	99	205	44	3	22	103	8	.394	78	139	.259
COLLINS, DAVE 86/27T, 87/148	1368	4484	612	1231	171	50	32	344	369	.356	422	594	.275
CONCEPCION, DAVE 87/731	2300	8247	950	2198	365	48	100	909	314	.359	690	1139	.267
COOPER, CECIL 87/10	1833	7099	987	2130	402	47	235	1089	88	.469	431	860	.300
CORRALES, PAT 87/268	300	767	63	166	28	3	4	54	1	.276	75	167	.216
COTTO, HENRY 87/174	174	282	39	74	9	0	2	20	13	.316	15	52	.262
CRUZ, JOSE 87/670	2189	7472	980	2147	372	90	153	1032	313	.423	854	958	.278
CRUZ, JULIO 87/790	1156	3859	557	916	113	27	23	279	343	.299	478	508	.237
DANIELS, KAL 87/466	74	181	34	58	10	4	6	23	15	.519	22	30	.320
DAULTON, DARREN 87/636	87	244	33	53	7	1	12	32	5	.402	55	79	.217
DAVIS, ALVIN 87/235	442	1624	224	457	85	5	63	266	6	.456	263	217	.281
DAVIS, CHILI 87/672	725	2648	352	715	122	19	75	342	79	.415	289	469	.270
DAVIS, ERIC 87/412	245	711	156	184	28	7	45	119	106	.508	99	187	.259
DAVIS, GLENN 87/560	276	985	148	260	48	3	54	173	3	.483	95	152	.264
DAVIS, JODY 87/270	777	2641	274	671	138	9	97	383	6	.423	226	505	.254
DAVIS, MIKE 87/83	649	2051	300	549	111	12	62	263	103	.424	153	356	.268
DAWSON, ANDRE 87/345	1443	5628	828	1575	295	67	225	838	253	.476	354	896	.280
DAYETT, BRIAN 87/369	121	249	25	61	12	1	9	43	0	.410	17	34	.245
DECINCES, DOUG 87/22	1512	5347	712	1397	287	29	221	815	55	.450	548	815	.261
DEER, ROB 86/31T, 87/547	225	652	102	142	22	4	44	109	6	.466	102	260	.218
DEMPSEY, RICK 87/28	1419	3949	438	939	183	12	78	380	17	.349	466	576	.238
DERNIER, BOB 87/715	636	1931	291	491	80	11	13	108	185	.327	180	235	.254
DIAZ, BO 87/41	718	2331	246	604	120	4	61	327	8	.393	166	308	.259
DIAZ, MIKE 87/469	103	216	24	58	10	0	12	37	0	.481	19	43	.269
DISTEFANO, BENNY 87/651	76	117	13	20	2	2	4	14	0	.325	6	18	.171
DODSON, PAT 87/449	767	2439	347	619	130	5	93	417	13	.426	492	579	.254
DORAN, BILL 87/472	620	2308	349	633	93	27	32	182	103	.380	308	273	.274
DOWNING, BRIAN 87/782	1586	5201	763	1382	235	17	166	734	40	.413	784	719	.266
DUNCAN, MARIANO 87/199	251	969	121	230	31	6	14	69	86	.325	68	191	.237
DUNSTON, SHAWON 87/346	224	831	106	210	48	7	21	86	24	.403	40	156	.253
DURHAM, LEON 87/290	862	3006	436	844	160	38	116	458	104	.475	377	551	.281
DWYER, JIM 87/246	1043	2128	304	543	95	16	56	268	20	.394	299	295	.255
DYKSTRA, LEN 87/295	230	667	117	187	36	10	9	64	46	.405	88	79	.280
EASLER, MIKE 86/33T, 87/135	1053	3400	445	1000	179	25	113	491	19	.461	301	644	.294
ESASKY, NICK 87/13	425	1367	167	326	58	12	55	198	10	.419	167	401	.238
ESPINO, JUAN 87/239	49	73	2	16	2	0	1	8	0	.288	3	15	.219
ESPINOZA, ALVARO 87/529	70	99	9	24	3	0	0	10	0	.273	2	19	.242
EVANS, DARRELL 87/265	2286	7761	1175	1947	294	35	347	1152	91	.432	1380	1191	.251
EVANS, DWIGHT 87/3, 87/645	1933	6661	1082	1785	361	57	291	949	61	.470	989	1289	.268
FELDER, MIKE 87/352	59	211	32	48	3	4	1	13	20	.294	18	22	.227
FELSKE, JOHN 87/443	54	104	7	14	3	1	1	9	0	.212	9	35	.135
FERNANDEZ, TONY 87/485	427	1518	196	448	70	23	15	137	43	.401	89	110	.295
FIELDER, CECIL 87/178	64	157	13	36	6	0	8	29	0	.420	12	43	.229
FISCHLIN, MIKE 87/434	516	941	109	207	29	6	3	68	24	.273	92	142	.220

Batting Record & Index

PLAYER	G	AB	R	H	2B	3B	HR	RBI	SB	SLG	BB	SO	AVG
FISK, CARLTON 87/756	1827	6521	1003	1767	316	42	281	977	115	.462	619	1006	.271
FITZGERALD, MIKE 87/212	301	884	66	209	35	3	14	106	9	.330	92	166	.236
FLANNERY, TIM 87/763	714	1897	207	493	62	20	9	162	15	.328	198	211	.260
FLETCHER, SCOTT 86/36T, 87/462	559	1619	218	426	75	14	11	149	33	.347	163	183	.263
FOLEY, TOM 87/78	366	888	83	220	40	8	9	82	16	.341	86	124	.248
FORD, CURT 87/399	96	226	32	59	17	2	2	32	14	.381	27	30	.261
FRANCO, JULIO 87/160	634	2482	330	715	110	22	27	326	74	.383	158	262	.288
FRANCONA, TERRY 86/37T, 87/785	451	1075	96	307	51	5	9	96	8	.367	42	69	.286
FREGOSI, JIM 86/39T, 87/318	1902	6523	844	1726	264	78	151	706	76	.398	715	1097	.265
GAETTI, GARY 87/710	790	2862	361	728	149	12	107	401	45	.427	224	512	.254
GAGNE, GREG 87/558	282	793	102	187	38	9	14	80	22	.359	50	171	.236
GALARRAGA, ANDRES 86/40T, 87/272	129	396	48	101	14	0	12	46	7	.381	33	97	.255
GANTNER, JIM 87/108	1120	3871	450	1066	155	23	40	367	63	.358	241	326	.275
GARCIA, DAMASO 87/395	931	3651	461	1046	173	26	32	301	197	.374	112	292	.286
GARNER, PHIL 87/304	1732	5885	751	1543	290	82	104	714	219	.392	535	795	.262
GARVEY, STEVE 87/100	2305	8759	1138	2583	438	43	271	1299	83	.448	478	993	.295
GEDMAN, RICH 87/740	656	2131	244	583	133	12	69	288	3	.444	150	322	.274
GIBSON, KIRK 87/765	765	2723	433	750	115	32	126	420	140	.480	309	596	.275
GLADDEN, DANNY 87/46	348	1258	196	353	50	11	16	110	94	.376	117	185	.281
GREENWELL, MIKE 87/259	48	66	11	21	3	0	4	12	1	.545	8	11	.318
GRICH, BOB 87/677	2008	6890	1033	1833	320	47	224	864	104	.424	1087	1278	.266
GRIFFEY, KEN 86/41T, 87/711	1678	6126	983	1839	315	73	121	707	189	.435	600	750	.300
GRIFFIN, ALFREDO 87/111	1228	4408	501	1133	160	63	19	336	135	.335	194	391	.257
GROSS, GREG 87/702	1537	3404	423	993	125	45	6	287	39	.360	471	229	.292
GRUBB, JOHNNY 87/384	1365	4040	544	1130	201	29	97	462	27	.416	551	542	.280
GRUBER, KELLY 87/458	107	172	21	32	4	1	6	18	2	.326	5	35	.186
GUERRERO, PEDRO 87/360	825	2842	448	865	137	21	139	461	75	.514	318	493	.304
GUILLEN, OZZIE 87/89	309	1038	129	271	40	13	3	80	15	.333	24	88	.261
GUTIERREZ, JACKIE 87/276	320	879	98	208	20	5	4	54	25	.284	31	114	.237
GWYNN, TONY 87/530	612	2364	352	770	107	26	27	230	99	.427	193	128	.326
HAIRSTON, JERRY 87/685	788	1568	202	408	83	6	25	185	4	.369	257	215	.260
HALL, MEL 87/51	440	1416	210	398	85	13	47	203	15	.459	136	277	.281
HAMILTON, JEFF 87/266	71	147	22	33	5	0	5	19	0	.361	2	43	.224
HARPER, TERRY 87/49	473	1337	135	339	49	5	32	163	36	.369	128	229	.254
HARRAH, TOBY 87/152	2155	7402	1115	1954	307	40	195	918	238	.395	1153	868	.264
HASSEY, RON 87/667	793	2331	249	658	121	7	50	322	10	.405	274	233	.282
HATCHER, BILLY 86/45T, 87/578	188	591	80	149	27	5	8	46	42	.355	31	64	.252
HATCHER, MICKEY 87/504	762	2543	269	715	133	16	28	270	8	.379	118	182	.281
HAYES, VON 87/666	779	2728	399	753	145	22	69	366	153	.421	286	388	.276
HEARN, ED 87/433	49	136	16	36	5	0	4	10	0	.390	12	19	.265
HEARRON, JEFF 87/274	16	30	2	6	1	0	0	4	0	.233	3	9	.200
HEATH, MIKE 86/46T, 87/492	853	2818	316	698	113	20	55	325	38	.361	189	375	.248
HEEP, DANNY 87/241	560	1313	144	338	71	5	25	149	9	.376	153	175	.257
HENDERSON, DAVE 87/452	690	2174	285	555	117	12	80	274	26	.431	186	454	.255
HENDERSON, RICKEY 87/311, 87/735	1087	4071	862	1182	188	39	103	417	660	.432	708	562	.290
HENDRICK, GEORGE 87/725	1914	6840	915	1910	332	27	259	1067	59	.449	546	975	.279
HERNANDEZ, KEITH 87/350	1721	6090	969	1840	372	58	128	900	96	.445	917	795	.302
HERNDON, LARRY 87/298	1372	4478	557	1222	168	74	94	483	91	.406	307	721	.273
HERR, TOM 87/721	873	3162	422	874	150	31	16	349	130	.359	359	322	.276
HERZOG, WHITEY 87/243	634	1614	213	414	60	20	25	172	13	.365	241	261	.257
HILL, DONNIE 87/339	357	1064	123	290	42	4	11	108	15	.351	55	104	.273
HOFFMAN, GLENN 87/374	657	1872	223	462	95	9	22	191	5	.342	123	264	.247
HORNER, BOB 87/660	960	3571	545	994	160	7	215	652	14	.508	337	489	.278
HOWELL, JACK 87/422	106	288	45	68	18	2	9	39	3	.406	35	61	.236
HOWSER, DICK 87/18	789	2483	398	617	90	17	16	165	105	.318	367	186	.248
HREBEK, KENT 87/679	761	2816	405	815	156	15	117	474	11	.480	319	415	.289
HUBBARD, GLENN 87/745	1055	3573	429	866	163	18	59	365	31	.348	410	513	.242

PLAYER	G	AB	R	H	2B	3B	HR	RBI	SB	SLG	BB	SO	AVG
HULETT, TIM 87/566	305	927	106	227	35	9	22	81	11	.373	52	176	.245
HURDLE, CLINT 87/317	512	1388	161	359	81	12	32	193	1	.403	176	260	.259
INCAVIGLIA, PETE 86/48T, 87/550	153	540	82	135	21	2	30	88	3	.463	55	185	.250
IORG, DANE 86/49T, 87/690	743	1647	149	455	103	11	14	216	5	.378	107	180	.276
IORG, GARTH 87/751	809	2140	216	568	114	16	16	208	20	.356	93	246	.265
JACKSON, BO 86/50T, 87/170	53	184	30	51	9	3	7	25	3	.473	22	81	.277
JACKSON, REGGIE 87/300, 87/312	2705	9528	1509	2510	449	48	548	1659	226	.493	1342	2500	.263
JACOBY, BROOK 87/405	460	1646	219	452	75	10	44	208	7	.413	136	334	.275
JAVIER, STAN 87/263	66	121	14	24	8	0	0	8	8	.264	16	28	.198
JELTZ, STEVE 87/294	275	711	68	148	15	7	1	56	9	.253	99	165	.208
JOHNSON, CLIFF 87/663	1369	3945	539	1016	198	10	196	699	9	.462	568	719	.258
JOHNSON, DAVE A. 87/543	1435	4797	564	1252	242	18	136	609	33	.404	559	675	.261
JOHNSON, HOWARD 87/267	411	1185	145	299	51	5	40	154	31	.405	128	249	.252
JOHNSON, WALLACE 87/588	135	227	23	56	3	4	1	20	12	.308	19	19	.247
JONES, RUPPERT 87/53	1246	4223	618	1056	207	36	139	551	141	.415	514	779	.250
JONES, TRACY 87/146	46	86	16	30	3	0	2	10	7	.453	9	5	.349
JOYNER, WALLY 86/51T, 87/80	154	593	82	172	27	3	22	100	5	.457	57	58	.290
KARKOVICE, RON 87/491	37	97	13	24	7	0	4	13	1	.443	9	37	.247
KEARNEY, BOB 87/498	455	1309	126	308	62	2	27	132	9	.348	66	226	.235
KELLY, TOM 87/618	No major league statistics											
KENNEDY, TERRY 87/540	962	3373	347	916	177	10	82	477	3	.403	238	565	.272
KHALIFA, SAMMY 87/164	159	471	38	104	20	3	2	35	5	.289	53	84	.221
KINGERY, MIKE 87/203	62	209	25	54	8	5	3	14	7	.388	12	30	.258
KINGMAN, DAVE 87/709	1941	6677	901	1575	240	25	442	1210	85	.478	608	1816	.236
KITTLE, RON 87/584	536	1770	238	408	61	3	115	299	16	.463	157	501	.231
KNIGHT, RAY 87/488	1240	3967	410	1102	230	25	67	497	13	.399	284	459	.278
KRENCHICKI, WAYNE 86/55T, 87/774	550	1063	107	283	44	6	15	124	7	.359	106	141	.266
KRUK, JOHN 86/56T, 87/123	122	278	33	86	16	2	4	38	2	.424	45	58	.309
LACY, LEE 87/182	1436	4291	615	1240	194	39	84	430	182	.411	340	608	.289
LAGA, MIKE 86/59T, 87/321	90	247	25	58	15	0	11	36	1	.429	16	74	.235
LAKE, STEVE 87/84	157	326	26	72	12	1	6	39	1	.319	8	41	.221
LANDREAUX, KEN 87/699	1149	3919	505	1062	176	45	85	456	140	.404	283	393	.271
LANDRUM, TITO 87/288	513	854	105	219	36	11	12	99	15	.367	71	160	.256
LANIER, HAL 86/60T, 87/343	1196	3703	297	843	111	20	8	273	11	.275	136	436	.228
LANSFORD, CARNEY 87/678	1139	4478	634	1307	212	30	113	563	108	.428	319	524	.292
LARKIN, BARRY 87/648	41	159	27	45	4	3	3	19	8	.403	9	21	.283
LARUSSA, TONY 87/68	132	176	15	35	5	2	0	7	0	.250	23	37	.199
LASORDA, TOM 87/493	No major league statistics											
LAUDNER, TIM 87/478	404	1136	129	256	61	2	42	139	1	.393	106	319	.225
LAVALLIERE, MIKE 87/162	128	344	20	76	11	2	3	36	0	.291	45	42	221
LAW, RUDI 86/62T, 87/382	749	2421	379	656	101	37	18	199	228	.366	184	210	.271
LAW, VANCE 87/127	724	2268	279	566	108	19	41	257	23	.368	246	361	.250
LAWLESS, TOM 87/647	196	359	43	81	13	1	1	17	33	.276	24	58	.226
LEACH, RICK 86/63T, 87/716	426	912	102	234	47	7	12	96	6	.363	80	112	.257
LEE, MANNY 87/574	99	118	17	24	0	1	1	7	1	.246	6	19	.203
LEMON, CHET 87/739	1467	5150	747	1429	302	48	166	666	53	.451	526	745	.277
LEONARD, JEFFREY 87/280	862	2964	379	808	127	31	81	428	120	.418	221	618	.273
LEYLAND, JIM 86/66T, 87/93	No major league statistics											
LOPES, DAVE 87/4, 87/445	1765	6311	1019	1661	230	50	154	608	555	.389	820	844	.263
LOWRY, DWIGHT 87/483	88	195	29	57	6	0	5	25	0	.400	20	30	.292
LYNN, FRED 87/370	1537	5589	906	1632	336	40	241	926	64	.496	716	847	.292
LYONS, STEVE 86/67T, 87/511	234	618	82	154	23	6	6	50	16	.335	51	111	.249
MADLOCK, BILL 87/734	1698	6207	859	1906	330	34	146	803	170	.442	571	460	.307
MAGADAN, DAVE 87/512	443	1530	271	495	90	11	4	234	6	.405	345	174	.324
MALDONADO, CANDY 86/69T, 87/335	429	950	99	231	53	5	29	138	5	.401	64	167	.243
MANNING, RICK 87/706	1458	5134	643	1323	182	42	56	445	164	.342	459	598	.258
MARSHALL, MIKE 87/664	575	1928	246	516	88	3	90	288	20	.456	161	474	.268

Batting Record & Index

PLAYER	G	AB	R	H	2B	3B	HR	RBI	SB	SLG	BB	SO	AVG
MARTINEZ, CARMELO 87/348	441	1335	164	333	69	3	49	179	2	.416	194	229	.249
MATTHEWS, GARY 87/390	1944	6986	1070	1972	315	51	231	955	183	.441	921	1092	.282
MATTINGLY, DON 87/500	572	2223	349	737	160	11	93	401	3	.539	171	141	.332
MATUSZEK, LEN 87/457	363	805	113	191	40	5	30	119	8	.411	87	164	.237
MAUCH, GENE 87/518	304	737	93	176	25	7	5	62	6	.312	104	82	.239
MAZZILLI, LEE 87/198	1243	3758	514	987	176	23	84	406	183	.389	555	562	.263
MCDOWELL, ODIBE 87/95	265	978	168	249	38	12	36	91	58	.428	101	197	.255
MCGEE, WILLIE 87/440	691	2703	379	806	101	52	32	311	181	.410	138	404	.298
MCGWIRE, MARK 87/366	18	53	10	10	1	0	3	9	0	.377	4	18	.189
MCNAMARA, JOHN 87/368	No major league statistics												
MCRAE, HAL 87/573	2066	7186	935	2081	481	66	190	1088	109	.454	643	778	.290
MEACHAM, BOBBY 87/62	333	1053	156	244	38	7	3	86	45	.290	107	221	.232
MELVIN, BOB 87/549	130	350	34	78	18	3	5	29	3	.334	18	90	.223
MERCADO, ORLANDO 87/514	151	375	23	78	15	4	3	34	3	.293	24	57	.208
MICHAEL, GENE 86/73T, 87/43	973	2806	249	642	86	12	15	226	22	.284	234	421	.229
MILLER, DARRELL 87/337	101	146	19	38	4	2	2	12	0	.356	9	27	.260
MILNER, EDDIE 87/253	680	2130	335	544	96	28	38	174	133	.380	258	238	.255
MITCHELL, KEVIN 86/74T, 87/653	115	342	51	94	22	2	12	44	3	.456	33	64	.275
MIZEROCK, JOHN 87/408	92	204	23	37	9	2	2	22	0	.275	38	39	.181
MOLITOR, PAUL 87/741	1010	4139	676	1203	200	45	79	390	231	.418	364	515	.291
MOORE, CHARLIE 87/676	1283	3926	441	1029	177	42	35	401	51	.355	333	458	.262
MORELAND, KEITH 87/177	887	3082	363	880	142	13	83	477	20	.421	295	353	.286
MORENO, OMAR 86/75T, 87/214	1382	4992	699	1257	171	87	37	386	487	.343	387	885	.252
MORMAN, RUSS 87/233	49	159	18	40	5	0	4	17	1	.358	16	36	.252
MORRIS, JOHN 87/211	39	100	8	24	0	1	1	14	6	.290	7	15	.240
MORRISON, JIM 87/237	884	2744	302	730	140	14	97	351	40	.433	174	411	.266
MOSEBY, LLOYD 87/210	974	3558	513	928	173	46	102	471	161	.421	351	697	.261
MOSES, JOHN 87/284	270	670	89	167	26	6	4	48	47	.324	54	103	.249
MOTLEY, DARRYL 87/99	407	1325	156	324	60	10	44	158	19	.405	67	185	.245
MULLINKS, RANCE 87/537	822	2288	295	614	150	12	43	273	11	.401	269	340	.268
MUMPHREY, JERRY 86/76T, 87/372	1404	4618	616	1330	196	53	57	522	173	.390	436	625	.288
MURPHY, DALE 87/490	1360	5017	813	1388	214	32	266	822	129	.491	617	1094	.277
MURPHY, DWAYNE 87/743T	1131	3828	575	948	122	20	145	528	95	.404	636	822	.248
MURRAY, EDDIE 87/120	1499	5624	884	1679	296	20	275	1015	55	.505	709	769	.299
NARRON, JERRY 87/474	388	832	64	177	23	2	21	96	0	.321	67	125	.213
NETTLES, GRAIG 87/205	2508	8716	1172	2172	316	27	384	1267	31	.424	1057	1165	.249
NEWMAN, AL 87/323	120	214	30	42	4	0	1	9	13	.229	24	24	.196
NICHOLS, REID 87/539	463	1013	134	269	55	6	18	111	25	.385	85	136	.266
NIETO, TOM 87/416	158	404	27	94	17	3	4	53	0	.319	37	76	.233
NIXON, OTIS 86/80T, 87/486	271	362	85	79	8	1	3	18	57	.271	30	55	.218
O'BRIAN, PETE 87/17	631	2235	278	602	111	14	75	328	18	.432	273	239	.269
O'MALLEY, TOM 87/154	316	937	88	238	37	5	9	95	2	.333	104	116	.254
OBERKFELL, KEN 87/627	1059	3423	408	970	169	36	20	303	54	.371	414	253	.283
OESTER, RON 87/172	980	3368	377	895	149	26	39	284	36	.360	296	530	.266
OGILVIE, BEN 87/586	1754	5913	784	1615	277	33	235	901	87	.450	560	852	.273
OQUENDO, JOSE 86/82T, 87/133	277	655	72	153	16	1	1	40	20	.266	49	106	.234
ORSULAK, JOE 87/414	298	876	126	238	34	14	2	44	51	.349	55	74	.272
ORTA, JORGE 87/738	1734	5779	730	1610	263	63	128	741	79	.412	497	707	.279
ORTIZ, JUNIOR 87/583	192	481	33	127	17	0	1	42	3	.306	22	82	.264
OWEN, SPIKE 87/591	504	1716	211	403	63	24	12	146	41	.321	155	185	.239
PACIOREK, TOM 86/83T, 87/729	1365	4061	488	1145	229	30	83	491	55	.414	244	685	.282
PAGLIARULO, MIKE 87/195	354	1085	150	259	55	8	54	167	4	.453	114	252	.239
PALMEIRO, RAFAEL 87/634	212	788	100	239	51	6	17	146	24	.448	85	66	.303
PANKOVITS, JIM 87/249	198	366	42	97	16	1	6	35	4	.363	30	74	.265
PARKER, DAVE 87/691	1779	6727	978	2024	397	69	247	1093	140	.491	495	1072	.301
PARRISH, LANCE 87/779	1146	4273	577	1123	201	23	212	700	22	.469	335	847	.263
PARRISH, LARRY 87/629	1619	5829	739	1552	324	31	210	840	27	.441	452	1094	.266

PLAYER	G	AB	R	H	2B	3B	HR	RBI	SB	SLG	BB	SO	AVG
PASQUA, DAN 87/74	162	428	61	113	20	1	25	70	2	.491	63	116	.264
PENA, TONY 87/60	801	2872	307	821	140	15	63	340	42	.411	174	372	.286
PENDLETON, TERRY 87/8	375	1399	149	357	58	11	7	161	61	.327	87	166	.255
PERRY, GERALD 87/639	288	694	85	176	21	2	13	77	24	.346	97	74	.254
PETRALLI, GANO 87/388	136	288	27	78	13	3	2	30	4	.358	18	33	.271
PETTIS, GARY 87/278	451	1469	247	369	46	21	12	126	162	.336	198	389	.251
PHELPS, KEN 87/333	371	911	150	214	32	6	64	156	7	.494	187	245	.235
PHILLIPS, TONY 87/188	502	1546	226	397	64	15	17	149	46	.351	191	298	.257
PINIELLA, LOU 86/86T, 87/168	1747	5867	651	1705	305	41	102	766	33	.409	368	541	.291
PORTER, DARRELL 86/88T, 87/689	1697	5409	746	1338	234	48	181	805	39	.409	875	982	.247
PRESLEY, JIM 87/45	380	1437	181	377	78	6	65	227	3	.461	82	335	.262
PRYOR, GREG 87/761	789	1883	204	471	85	9	14	146	11	.327	104	185	.250
PUCKETT, KIRBY 87/450	450	1928	262	587	78	24	35	201	55	.424	91	255	.304
PUHL, TERRY 87/693	1155	4086	579	1150	188	50	57	363	184	.394	406	413	.281
PYZNARSKI, TIM 87/429	566	1809	326	514	99	20	74	302	76	.484	284	473	.284
QUINONES, LUIS 87/362	90	148	18	27	3	4	0	15	4	.257	4	21	.182
QUINONES, REY 86/89T, 87/561	98	312	32	68	16	1	2	22	4	.295	24	57	.218
QUIRK, JAMIE 87/354	534	1188	100	286	58	4	23	125	3	.354	63	228	.241
RAINES, TIM 87/30	882	3372	604	1028	180	55	48	314	461	.434	469	376	.305
RAMIREZ, RAFAEL 87/76	871	3358	365	882	127	21	36	280	87	.345	165	370	.263
RAMOS, DOMINGO 87/641	250	517	50	108	16	0	3	33	5	.257	42	67	.209
RANDOLPH, WILLIE 87/701	1494	5511	897	1511	216	55	39	451	233	.355	875	454	.274
RAY, JOHNNY 87/747	808	3053	366	880	183	23	32	327	64	.395	218	171	.288
RAYFORD, FLOYD 87/426	370	994	107	244	43	1	36	114	4	.399	53	216	.245
REDUS, GARY 86/90T, 87/42	459	1516	284	376	80	22	42	141	171	.413	219	333	.248
REED, JEFF 87/247	93	196	18	44	9	1	2	10	1	.311	18	28	.224
REYNOLDS, CRAIG 87/779	1177	3742	409	968	115	62	35	321	49	.351	170	321	.259
REYNOLDS, HAROLD 87/91	222	618	72	129	26	6	1	31	34	.275	48	66	.209
REYNOLDS, R. J. 87/109	319	1034	136	278	57	11	16	125	46	.392	79	176	.269
REYNOLDS, RONN 87/471	97	239	16	49	7	0	3	13	0	.272	14	61	.205
RICE, JIM 87/480	1790	7127	1104	2163	331	74	351	1289	55	.518	564	1218	.303
RILES, EARNIE 87/523	261	974	123	260	36	9	14	92	9	.366	89	134	.267
RIPKEN, CAL 87/784	830	3210	529	927	183	20	133	472	11	.483	313	417	.289
ROBERTS, BIP 86/91T, 87/637	101	241	34	61	5	2	1	12	14	.303	14	29	.253
ROBIDOUX, BILLY JO 86/92T, 87/401	74	232	20	50	10	0	4	29	0	.310	45	52	.216
RODGERS, BOB 87/293	932	3033	259	704	114	18	31	288	17	.312	234	409	.232
ROENICKE, GARY 86/94T, 87/683	947	2443	331	611	122	4	111	375	16	.440	366	390	.250
ROENICKE, RON 87/329	450	961	128	238	47	2	16	104	23	.351	172	172	.248
ROMERO, ED 86/95T, 87/675	511	1350	166	336	60	1	7	122	9	.310	106	108	.249
ROMINE, KEVIN 87/121	59	63	9	15	4	0	0	3	3	.302	4	13	.238
ROSE, PETE 87/200, 87/393	3562	14053	2165	4256	746	135	160	1314	198	.409	1566	1143	.303
ROWDON, WADE 87/569	47	96	11	24	5	1	0	12	2	.323	11	19	.250
ROYSTER, JERRY 87/403	1287	3910	518	979	149	33	33	324	185	.331	382	486	.250
RUSSELL, BILL 87/116	2181	7318	796	1926	293	57	46	627	167	.338	483	667	.263
RUSSELL, JOHN 87/379	213	630	68	151	41	3	24	94	2	.429	55	208	.240
SALAS, MARK 87/87	225	638	80	170	28	9	17	75	3	.418	36	72	.266
SALAZAR, ARGENIS 86/96T, 87/533	233	509	41	108	25	5	0	37	2	.281	12	93	.212
SALAZAR, LUIS 87/454	651	2136	232	565	79	24	39	232	103	.379	84	358	.265
SAMPLE, BILLY 86/98T, 87/114	826	2516	371	684	127	9	46	230	98	.384	195	230	.272
SAMUEL, JUAN 87/255	484	2020	310	541	104	46	52	226	170	.442	91	467	.268
SANDBERG, RYNE 87/680	790	3146	494	902	153	39	74	343	189	.431	242	447	.287
SANTANA, RAFAEL 87/378	374	1089	94	267	41	2	3	71	1	.295	76	116	.245
SAX, STEVE 87/769	774	3070	420	872	118	24	19	230	211	.357	274	294	.284
SCHMIDT, MIKE 87/430	2107	7292	1347	1954	352	57	495	1392	169	.536	1354	1748	.268
SCHOFIELD, DICK 87/502	447	1350	160	298	48	12	28	123	39	.336	122	212	.221
SCHROEDER, BILL 87/302	201	694	86	160	30	1	32	76	1	.415	32	197	.231
SCHU, RICK 87/209	221	653	98	170	33	6	17	54	10	.407	62	128	.260

PLAYER	G	AB	R	H	2B	3B	HR	RBI	SB	SLG	BB	SO	AVG
SCIOSCIA, MIKE 87/144	665	1968	181	519	91	6	26	199	11	.356	288	130	.264
SHEETS, LARRY 87/552	233	682	88	185	26	1	36	112	2	.471	50	111	.271
SHELBY, JOHN 87/208	491	1354	188	325	50	13	30	135	52	.363	63	260	.240
SHEPARD, RON 87/643	115	108	23	18	6	0	2	5	3	.278	5	37	.167
SHERIDAN, PAT 87/234	426	1257	166	329	54	9	24	125	51	.376	105	251	.262
SIERRA, RUBEN 87/6, 87/261	113	382	50	101	13	10	16	55	7	.476	22	65	.264
SIMMONS, TED 86/102T, 87/516	2305	8396	1048	2402	469	47	242	1348	20	.440	819	662	.286
SKINNER, JOEL 87/626	185	450	38	108	15	2	6	46	2	.322	28	116	.240
SLAUGHT, DON 87/308	447	1457	156	405	80	13	28	159	11	.408	76	194	.278
SMALLEY, ROY 87/744	1543	5348	713	1369	228	24	155	660	25	.395	735	856	.256
SMITH, LONNIE 87/69	909	3148	571	915	166	37	41	289	299	.406	326	458	.291
SMITH, OZZIE 87/749	1317	4739	583	1169	179	38	13	374	303	.309	528	305	.247
SNYDER, CORY 87/192	103	416	58	113	21	1	24	69	2	.500	16	123	.272
SPEIER, CHRIS 87/424	2039	6631	698	1634	276	49	98	661	35	.347	777	889	.246
SPILMAN, HARRY 87/64	401	639	80	151	25	0	16	97	0	.351	61	95	.236
STAPLETON, DAVE 87/507	582	2028	238	550	118	8	41	224	6	.398	114	162	.271
STEFERO, JOHN 87/563	61	131	16	33	3	0	2	17	0	.321	19	27	.252
STILLWELL, KURT 86/104T, 87/623	104	279	31	64	6	1	0	26	6	.258	26	30	.229
STONE, JEFF 87/532	230	702	97	209	14	15	10	48	65	.403	44	129	.298
STRAWBERRY, DARRYL 87/460	516	1810	292	471	84	20	108	343	100	.508	267	496	.260
STUBBS, FRANKLIN 86/105T, 87/292	229	646	77	139	13	4	31	77	9	.392	61	173	.215
SULLIVAN, MARC 87/66	77	200	26	40	6	0	3	18	0	.275	14	49	.200
SUNDBERG, JIM 87/190	1763	5590	578	1397	229	35	83	579	20	.348	644	854	.250
SURHOFF, B.J. 87/216				No major league statistics									
SVEUM, DALE 86/106T, 87/327	91	317	35	78	13	2	7	35	4	.366	33	63	.246
TABLER, PAT 87/575	575	1966	250	566	98	16	29	252	8	.398	178	301	.288
TANNER, CHUCK 86/107T, 87/593	396	885	98	231	39	5	21	105	2	.388	82	93	.261
TARTABULL, DANNY 86/108T, 87/476	166	592	87	164	33	7	28	110	5	.498	71	174	.277
TEMPLETON, GARRY 87/325	1423	5562	703	1578	240	86	44	519	215	.382	256	773	.284
TETTLETON, MICKEY 87/649	201	498	59	116	23	1	14	55	9	.367	78	131	.233
TEUFEL, TIM 86/109T, 87/158	409	1359	180	355	81	8	31	148	6	.401	158	193	.261
THOMAS, ANDRES 86/111T, 87/296	117	341	32	86	17	2	6	34	4	.367	8	51	.252
THOMAS, GORMAN 87/495	1435	4677	681	1051	212	13	268	782	50	.448	697	1339	.225
THOMPSON, MILT 86/112T, 87/409	194	580	71	160	15	3	8	33	42	.353	44	109	.276
THOMPSON, ROBBY 86/113T, 87/658	149	549	73	149	27	3	7	47	12	.370	42	112	.271
THON, DICKIE 87/386	649	2079	258	565	99	24	32	192	98	.389	162	275	.272
THORNTON, ANDRE 87/780	1529	5206	784	1332	242	22	253	890	47	.457	866	826	.256
TOLLESON, WAYNE 86/115T, 87/224	568	1700	217	433	48	14	7	93	96	.312	146	256	.255
TRABER, JIM 87/484	75	233	31	59	7	0	13	46	0	.451	20	35	.253
TRAMMELL, ALAN 87/687	1289	4631	702	1300	214	42	90	504	149	.403	488	519	.281
TREVINO, ALEX 86/116T, 87/173	672	1876	192	467	81	8	15	186	13	.325	161	231	.249
TRILLO, MANNY 86/117T, 87/732	1580	5533	553	1450	226	33	52	531	54	.343	417	664	.262
UPSHAW, WILLIE 87/245	965	3198	470	857	155	38	97	420	66	.431	332	496	.268

PLAYER	G	AB	R	H	2B	3B	HR	RBI	SB	SLG	BB	SO	AVG
URIBE, JOSE 87/633	312	948	96	218	35	5	6	72	31	.296	91	135	.230
VALENTINE, BOBBY 87/118	639	1698	176	441	59	9	12	157	27	.326	140	134	.260
VAN SLYKE, ANDY 87/33	521	1512	205	392	79	22	41	204	104	.422	203	274	.259
VENABLE, MAX 87/226	525	961	117	222	36	12	11	80	57	.328	84	141	.231
VIRGIL, OZZIE 86/119T, 87/571	497	1493	176	359	60	5	61	202	2	.410	175	312	.240
WALKER, CHICO 87/695	81	194	32	49	3	4	2	16	19	.340	17	38	.253
WALKER, GREG 87/397	506	1649	211	453	95	16	73	280	16	.485	138	270	.275
WALKER, TONY 87/24	84	90	19	20	7	0	2	10	11	.367	11	15	.222
WALLACH, TIM 87/55	839	3031	338	771	156	15	110	406	26	.425	239	472	.254
WALLING, DENNY 87/222	903	2133	287	594	95	24	41	294	37	.403	227	219	.278
WARD, GERY 87/762	831	3118	444	900	144	36	92	419	71	.446	240	524	.289
WASHINGTON, CLAUDELL 86/122T, 87/15	1529	5488	762	1524	275	61	130	665	270	.421	386	1029	.278
WASHINGTON, RON 87/169	462	1277	152	340	47	19	17	119	25	.373	55	212	.266
WEAVER, EARL 87/568				No major league statistics									
WEBSTER, MITCH 87/442	266	822	132	232	41	16	19	83	51	.440	79	119	.282
WHITAKER, LOU 87/661	1283	4705	724	1320	202	49	93	522	95	.404	576	575	.281
WHITE, DEVON 87/139	50	58	15	13	1	1	1	3	9	.328	7	11	.224
WHITE, FRANK 87/692	1803	6100	743	1583	314	53	131	693	166	.393	300	798	.260
WHITT, ERNIE 87/698	835	2303	266	571	107	11	86	323	13	.416	248	312	.248
WILFONG, ROB 87/251	947	2682	316	667	97	23	38	259	53	.345	204	385	.249
WILKERSON, CURT 87/228	408	1115	116	270	33	10	1	64	38	.292	57	182	.242
WILLARD, JERRY 87/137	266	707	77	179	28	1	21	99	1	.385	76	142	.253
WILLIAMS, DICK 86/124T, 87/418	1023	2959	358	768	157	12	70	331	12	.392	227	392	.260
WILLIAMS, JIMY 87/786				No major league statistics									
WILLIAMS, REGGIE 87/232	150	312	39	87	14	2	4	32	10	.375	23	61	.279
WILLS, MAURY 87/315	1942	7588	1067	2134	177	71	20	458	586	.331	552	684	.281
WILSON, GLENN 87/97	676	2358	265	636	130	19	58	316	22	.415	134	394	.270
WILSON, MOOKIE 87/625	800	3015	451	834	124	49	40	249	238	.390	168	497	.277
WILSON, WILLIE 87/783	1267	4908	775	1457	176	97	30	357	470	.391	249	661	.297
WINFIELD, DAVE 87/770	1964	7287	1135	2083	353	71	305	1234	195	.479	791	1040	.286
WINNINGHAM, HERM 87/141	229	524	58	125	13	9	7	37	34	.338	47	130	.239
WOHLFORD, JIM 87/527	1220	3049	349	793	125	33	21	305	89	.343	241	376	.260
WOODARD, MIKE 87/286	72	161	26	40	3	1	1	14	13	.298	14	12	.248
WRIGHT, GEORGE 86/128T	627	2160	231	529	88	18	42	208	19	.361	126	314	.245
WYNEGAR, BUTCH 87/464	1243	4183	486	1069	170	14	64	493	10	.349	609	408	.256
WYNNE, MARVELL 87/37	497	1644	198	408	65	18	16	120	57	.339	113	226	.248
YASTRZEMSKI, CARL 87/314	3308	11988	1816	3419	646	59	452	1844	168	.460	1845	1393	.285
YEAGER, STEVE 86/130T, 87/258	1269	3584	357	816	118	16	102	410	14	.355	342	726	.228
YOUNG, MIKE 87/309	410	1258	181	323	56	5	54	177	11	.438	157	313	.257
YOUNGBLOOD, JOEL 87/759	1180	3327	419	890	168	23	74	382	58	.399	304	538	.268
YOUNT, ROBIN 87/773	1811	7037	1043	2019	380	82	153	827	166	.429	535	780	.287
ZUVELLA, PAUL 86/131T, 87/102	118	269	20	57	10	1	0	7	2	.257	25	22	.212

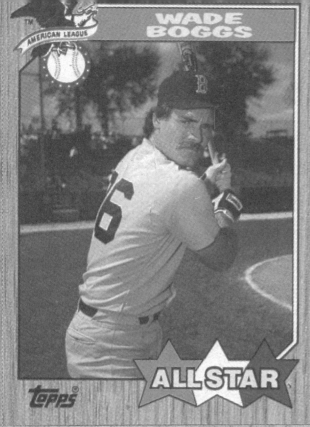

WADE BOGGS

ALL STAR

Topps

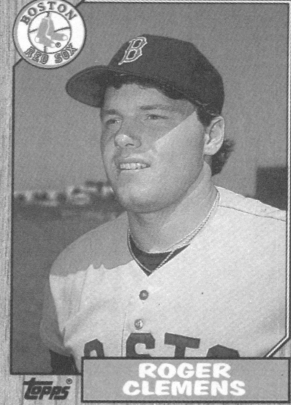

ROGER CLEMENS

Topps

MARK LANGSTON

Topps

MIKE SCOTT

Topps

MIKE SCHMIDT

ALL STAR

Topps

TIM RAINES

Topps

DAVE PARKER

ALL STAR

Topps

JESSE BARFIELD

Topps

VINCE COLEMAN

Topps